Pour giovanna
et Steven,

with

love !

Emmanuelle

ANGELINGS:
BOOK OF VALUES

FROM **SPIRIT** TO **BUSINESS**

a manual of creative integration

Emmanuelle Linard

www.angelings.com

ISBN: 978-0-9861951-1-2

Printed in the United States of America

First edition

CONTENTS

Preface

This book is the first brick in the foundation of an enterprise to help individuals and groups live a fuller life. This project will develop a set of tools for self-definition and networking to be used alongside our personal and professional creative evolution.

We live in exciting times.

More and more light is shed onto society as the flux of information through new media increases. Every bit of data coming to our attention requires processing, whether we choose to ignore it or to act upon it. As the global library grows, life places more demands on us; more choices have to be made on a regular basis, which is both stimulating and confusing. We need some clarity.

Through hardship, wisdom, or grace, an increasing number of us have come to realize that we now can—even must—choose to live in full compliance with our creative identity. Some of us still need to define what truly matters. Some of us have discovered the unique ingredients that make up the recipe for a fulfilling life and are ready to organize them before offering our rebranded selves to the world community.

This project aims at engaging people to define their creative identity and share their creative experiences through a network of like-minded people. It offers the possibility to precipitate constituents of our personality and reconcile our creative fragments; it encourages us to remember our passions and materialize our potential to experience a fuller life. Then, it invites us to engage in a creative conversation with others, to unite our teams and elaborate exciting projects.

For this, we need a guiding frame to define our talents and describe our strengths; we need a matchmaking engine to inspire each other.

This project applies to any field that touches our human existence— design, craft, trade, lifestyles, well-being, debate, activism, or indulgence, and so much more that we will think of in the future, as well as combinations of all of these. It starts an inner conversation about self-integration to help us find our purpose and shine on the world stage.

I wish to help build a path to cope and dance with the flux of unforeseen societal, environmental, technological, and economic changes, personally and professionally. A womb for creativity, a community for empowered individuals, a life management program, a personal and collective journal, a hub for entrepreneurs in the becoming, this project helps us manifest personal and collective dreams. It can take the shape of practical applications such as a digital platform, a software application, a coaching method, a database, or an organization.

Humbled by a task of this magnitude, looking up toward a goal so high that I cannot see its contour, I have to ask where it starts.

I realize that the ground layer for creative achievement is anchored in a solid base of values. We can blossom effortlessly when we are in synchronicity with our core ethics, while staying connected to the ever-changing collective mind.

This book describes a set of twelve fundamental concepts based on ancient wisdom that I believe are relevant to our contemporary living experience.

It is the first stage of an experiment, an intervention, a movement, a network, a method that evolves collectively into a service to the community.

But before anything, it is a practice.

I hope this open invitation will inspire you to join.

Thank you and happy reading,

Emmanuelle Linard

Manufesto

This book presents a snapshot of my values today. This reflection is personal. The surmises contained here engage only me, and are in constant evolution. They morph as I live and breathe.

I am inspired to explain what is driving me to turn my life around and invest time and energy in a new adventure. I walk my own talk as I write this material, for it helps me to refine my thoughts. This creative journaling process may even be inspirational to others some day. I do not know whether this enterprise will be successful, nor do I know what shape(s) it will take if it does succeed. I gladly take on the challenge and welcome surprises.

Writing doesn't come easy; yet I choose to enjoy it. Who would have thought? Alongside the investigation of the core values that have proven their worth to us throughout history I lose myself in the research. In my attempt to be fair and truthful to the reader about the data I present, I trace the slithering evolution of those fundamentals back to their source. Values are tricky; one day they seduce the masses, the next they revolt them. The more I learn, the less I know. It never fails: Just as I think I have it all figured out, as I finally put a satisfied period at the end of my synthesis, an unforeseen antithesis invites itself to the table of my prerogatives; I end up offering it *la place du pauvre,*[1] the vagrant's seat, as I should. The conversation starts again. But I must to draw the line. These many wonderful scholars, critics of critics before and ahead of us, will never cease to talk. Truth transcends the responsibility of a single point of view, and honestly this is a relief: the bridge between spirit and business is a long one, and if I want to cross it I won't take more time to stop and smell the flowers of academia. Going back to scholarship has been a pure joy, but now is the time to apply what I have learned so far.

The task at hand is giant, for I couldn't have picked two domains more unlikely to meet. On one end, the domain of work: materialistically rewarding, epicurean, fact-based; on the other end, that of spirit: hypothetical, idealistic, always extending its matterless hand for us earthlings to grab and ascend into enhanced versions of ourselves.

These two worlds don't interact much; corporate shrugs at utopian New Age, and New Age avoids greedy corporate. Yet both worlds have crowds of followers, some of whom are now realizing that each side has treasures to offer.

Before we take our first step toward each other we need some guarantees: business and spirituality equally need to revamp their image. Corporate has too many dirty secrets and needs to clean up its act. New Age is buried under esoteric words unrelated to everyday matters and sentimental visuals lacking an edge and a sense of humor.

This book presents common values around which folks can sit down and talk. In sum, it offers a bridge to many more bridges in construction, that will eventually mend the gap between our two homes, the home of what exists on earth and the home of what exists in the ether; between what is and what is not yet; between a dream life and the manifestation of it.

These values are alive; just as complex as the human psyche they reflect, they play tricks in each other's houses. The reader will notice that concepts echo from one value to the next. Yet they form a whole and each matters equally for the process of creative integration.

In a perfect world the structure of this material is circular: each chapter, strengthened by its own value, can be read independently. Yet books have to have a beginning and an end. The brain itself is trained to read in a linear fashion for simplification's sake. I kept my values in a row from 1 to 12. Numbers rule.

I chose to write in the English language for its conciseness. After all, those noble ancient values are, as I discover, deceptively simple.

Simplicity is an art. Brevity is a condition sine qua non for business in our age of speed and polyvalence. Being basic sounds like déjà-vu, and it is; the ritornelle of values has been sung so many times that it comes through one ear and goes out the other. It no longer leaves a dent on our reasoning process: precisely our problem. We forgot; we lost our ethics among the delicious complexity of our lifestyles and the creative intricacies of our work ways. Dodgy methods of success endorsing monetary wealth replaced ones based in values. But these ways benefit only a few at the top and certainly do not work in the long run. Today, we could use a reminder. Braving the trap of truisms, I choose to state the obvious.

This manuscript started as a necessity.

I am no stranger to the practice of journaling. I would start early in the morning at the corner coffee shop, typing on my laptop random thoughts. I quickly jotted down thousands of pages on "automatic pilot" that I lost when my hard drive crashed. It was no big deal, because I would never read them again anyway. Then, during the week of December 17, 2012, an unusually large body of inspiration came to me. My ideas needed sorting out. I had to lay them down, trusting that some clarity would come in the process. I started writing my thoughts, this time paying attention to spelling, sensing that they could be worth re-reading some day.

It felt like a dilly-dallying exercise in spirituality, philosophy and psychology, a crossbreed of spiritual psy-phi. I wondered if the content was developing into a project that would be useful to me one day, as well as to other individuals. It might possibly even be applicable to business practices.

Soon enough, I had to acquaint myself with a major paradox: This project wants to help us express our uniqueness through creativity in a global reality where everything is co-created. It is a serenade to both our singularity and our plurality, to the one within and to the many without, to the entrepreneur and to the collectivist.

No wonder it is a challenge to bridge spirit with business. How can we satisfy the self *and* the community? How can we be magicians *and* achievers? How can we turn the mirage into a miracle? Well, first, we need a solid sense of humor.

I'm a businessperson. I came to New York City from Paris in 1999 to start up a company with fashion and design trend forecaster Lidewij Edelkoort to distribute her publications. I like defining strategies to sell ideas, to develop great products, and to serve the community through creative education and teamwork. Following the quirks of the corporate game, I grew the business and sustained the company's high profile through the economic crises of 2001 and 2008.

Although I was successful at the corporate game, at the same time, I have always been drawn to mysticism. Like many children, I was mesmerized by fairies, wizards, and all things magic. I would wait in great anticipation for the next episodes of television series such as *The Sixth Sense, Kung-Fu, Bewitched,* or the French psychedelic cartoon *Barbapapa.* Later, I developed an interest in ancestral divination, which led me to start work in trend forecasting at the age of twenty. I have always been engaged in some form of spiritual activity: stargazing, imaginary friends, practicing yoga, movement channeling, or exploring parallel realities.

During my years as a consultant, I included elements gathered from my spiritual research in my lectures. It made my work more fun and my content more personal. Surprisingly, the input was well-received by my clients, including designers, marketers, brand strategists, and manufacturers. It was encouraging to see that people from different backgrounds were open to considering concepts of ancient wisdom to enhance their work and life experiences.

To keep the business afloat in a difficult market I was under pressure to devote the lion's share of my time to selling at all costs. I realized I was compromising my values. Sometimes the just way between heroic tenacity and naïve perseverance is to let go.

In a way, the struggle I went through to maintain the business in the aftermath of the economic crisis of 2008 served me well. I came to know there had to be more purpose to my life.

In 2014, I left my job and moved from the bustling pace of the city to a rural area. I wanted to reassess my principles, be 100 percent in agreement with myself, and create a tool to encourage others to express their creative identity.

We are all powerful creators channeling an omnipresent life force. Functionality is the instrument of life on earth; creativity is the goal. We can connect with our innate ability to craft a unique way of life according to our passions. We turn the invention that is fear into a stepping stone as we place joy at the forefront of our contingencies. We become aware enough to embrace our core ethics, and brave enough to venture with others into a new way of trading and bringing healthier dynamics to society, one individual at a time.

This is a reflection derived from personal exploration in matters of spirit and wisdom. It is my contribution to the global game of creative manifestation and ascension as a species to a more meaningful way to live. Ancient teachings have the power to federate people. I am interested in extracting the values that bring everyone to the same page, and defining an ideological intersection where a large number of people can coalesce. I sense that at this juncture, there is a recipe for self-improvement and successful business that cannot *not* work.

This project is an open question: What do we need to define our real selves and express our creativity? Can we inspire others with the way we transform our traumas into valuable lessons? Can we outline our dreams and share them in the purpose of manifesting them one day? Is there a path to self-knowing that works its charm and makes us feel that we belong, in our lives and jobs? Does this path lead the working community to a corporate sincerity that doesn't exist yet on a large scale? It is worth investigating.

This book is not a political statement against the corporate ways and top executive layers, but certain things need to be said to define constructive actions and to make us feel that we belong in this society. Politics is the science of public affairs. In that sense, any work pertaining to the welfare of citizens and the consequences of their actions for the collective domain is political. However, some of us politicians became artists in diplomacy or ambassadors of tricks. The art of politics is anchored in the philosophy of early antiquity.[2] Scholars were entrusted to organize community resources and the repartition of power to see to the fortune of all. Reserved to an educated elite, politics quickly became the centerpiece of one's career, creating leaders disconnected from everyday trade and the community's needs. The reality show of personality cults and non-pragmatic leaders infuriates many of us either into rebellion or aversion to election systems. Narcissism in politics rewards only a few; it is of no use to crowds. In truth, politics belongs to all and all can benefit from it. When we reestablish the link between politics and philosophy, we start questioning again, we fine-tune our thinking, and engage in constructive debate for the well-being of the many.

My research taught me much about ancient wisdom and philosophy. I discovered the language of philosophy to be more accessible than anticipated and an incredible tool to discuss new ways to build our communities. My intent isn't to trivialize ancient wisdom and philosophy. Rather, I wish to acknowledge that they are an intrinsic part of every decision we make and every action we take on a global level and that they fuel our intellectual metabolism with their truths. They help me greatly in my own course and I wish to share what I learned. This book is a recapitulation.

I am interested in assessing which positions can be adopted by a large number of people in order to design integrity-oriented communities.

Integrity comes as the sum of proven values that I propose to explore here to strengthen our personal belief structure and build faith in our creative abilities.

I hope that this material can start a group reflection and possibly the shaping of instruments for personal and social reinvention. If I do not yet see the whole shape of these instruments, I sense their presence in the collective potential. I am game to making them tangible; with your help, it will become clear. It will take the time it needs. With heart and focus I am committed to describing the information that comes to my awareness.

It is playing me as much as I am playing it, and it has a life on its own.

1

BE

Trusting Our Creative Identity

Truth, Focus, Creation

I sold publications for a while before I added consultancy to my daily services. I couldn't have sold the publications if they weren't beautiful, in form and in concept. I like marketing and communicating, both forms of exchange. I used my consulting skills to sell; engaging clients in creative conversations with educational workshops gave an additional dimension to my work. Coaching great people on how to gather information, decode the news, make deductions, and apply the results of this analysis to specific projects felt like a purposeful activity, suited to who I am. But part of me was missing.

Lost magic:

As far as I can remember, something was always missing. As a child I would watch the stars and the light they radiated light-years ago and wonder what they were emitting today that we weren't yet seeing. Distant, mysterious and magical, they seemed to outrun time while remaining present.

Every child is born with an innate and intimate connection with nature, elemental forces, and living beings. As the sense of self develops, the process of individuation[3] starts, allowing the child to differentiate itself from elements external to its body limits and from other people. Dissociation sets in, anchoring division in our physical reality. In a way, we learn to think from outside our core. From the first to the last breath, the mind rarely reaches a high form of remembering what German Idealist philosophers referred to as the *Absolute*, an unconditional, omnipresent and united concept to describe consciousness. Early on we leave behind our sense of belonging to Wuji[4] or unity, according to Taoist cosmology. We have trouble reconnecting with the vastness we came from. We abandon what Hinduism describes in Sanskrit as *Tat Tvam Asi, That Thou Art,*[5] the merging between the governing principle of Ultimate Reality and the self. We are taught young that estrangement from the absolute is realistic. We learn to steer clear of the dark and the unknown, and we are told that magic is an illusion.

A personal quest for spirituality:

As a child I wanted to be a post office clerk and a fairy. Developing the skills to do a bit of both, I ended up with a managing position in trend forecasting. I was grateful to my employer for offering me the opportunity to set up an antenna in New York. I could have a go at the American dream. Cultural France is skeptical toward spirituality. New America, land of opportunity, diversity, and a vast geography offering raw space for self-exploration, appeared to me a propitious place to develop my spiritual potential.

I did well in management and created a good life, but after a while I felt under-employed by the universe. I wanted to find an optimal way to serve the community while living my personal dream, voicing my passions, and being true to myself.

I looked for answers where I had started: amid the stars. I looked into the disciplines of astronomy and astrology, with their celestial names and myths. I inquired about various cultural interpretations of the laws of the universe, some of them empirical, a few arbitrary or esoteric, many old and wise, even life-changing. I traveled alone and far, seeking answers in the thick of jungles, in the silence of deserts, in the height of mountains, in natural and man-made temples. These were my spiritual activities. I was also a committed student in an athletic school of yoga; I have always had a regular physical practice of gymnastics, handball, or dance. It is vital to maintain an intimate connection with the body, our vehicle and closest friend on this earth plane.

At the age of 41, I was offered the opportunity to take an introductory class in meditation for one week. I wasn't thrilled, because the classes were scheduled in the early evening, happy hour time. Meditation and beer are not the best of buddies. I figured that I could refrain from socializing at the local bar for a week. What followed in the next few days was rather surprising. After my morning coffee, my heart started pounding faster, so I switched to tea. I also felt compelled to change to a less demanding form of yoga that included chanting and meditation. After that week, I didn't return to drinking beer, or any form of alcohol for that matter. Coffee, physical exertion, and alcohol left me. I might have a sip of beer once in a blue moon, or enjoy a class of power yoga to prove to myself that I can; but generally, these habits are gone, without effort on my part. To this day, I still haven't decided to quit any of these things.

Curiously, I didn't notice any modifications in my physical wellbeing; I usually enjoy a good amount of energy. But these changes certainly altered the way I interacted with society; I lost contact with most of my acquaintances. Self-work is a lonely journey that one must be prepared for, and I was ready.

Exploring paranormal fields of perception:

Over the years I experimented with out-of-body experiences, lucid dreaming, and intuitive channeling.[6] I started to practice hour-long meditations on a regular basis. I realized that my body had the ability to intercept some form of universal energy and could make me move slowly and smoothly without the conscious control of my mind. I became aware of my body's wisdom. I found these short trips in the great beyond so riveting that I followed through for about three months. I reached a point where my body was channeling movements at night while I slept. I lost weight, became twice as strong, blew up my hair dryer and a few light bulbs and froze up my computers upon touch. In a few instances, animals would only feel my presence when they approached closely, getting startled. My vibration level must have been altered. Except for a couple of unsavory encounters with immaterial beings, for the most part these experiences were happy and interesting. They proved to me that there is more to life than meets the mind.

I grew comfortable with perceiving visual or audible signals that weren't of this world and accepted their validity without demanding proof. I grew curious about coincidences. I hypothesized that synchronicities are logical consequences to/of each other, provided that the observer is standing far enough away to perceive the long threaded links between seemingly disconnected facts. I wanted to understand the whole picture.

I familiarized myself with a discourse where everything could be connected and plausible, where miracles are a common occurrence in a benevolent environment that seems to fulfill our desires, no matter how pleasant or challenging the experience turns out to be. I am an optimist: I find that we truly get what we ask for, and it is most encouraging. Everything is possible; if one person can fulfill his or her dreams, anyone can do it.

This experience of life between worlds was compelling but I decided that the beauty of my life was to be present in the here and now. I committed to physical reality, while bringing in what I had had a glance of.

My out-ventures gave me the vigor to interrupt my career, to pause and tap into my creativity to establish a bridge between these realms of perception.

Expansion is a living force:

Since the Big Bang started the universe on its expansion 13.8 billion years ago, basic atoms have fused and split their masses and charges to create new atoms ever more complex. The universe is a vessel in a constant state of expansion, and as we ride along physical reality, so are we. As without, so within; growth is an act of nature. Growth is the law, and comes as an innate setting with our human configuration, biologically, socially, and spiritually.

Every entity, every company is compelled to grow in one form or another, be it in size, in profit, in exposure, or in ethics.

Creating is our birthright:

As a civilization, we worked our way through the veil of obscurantism over the ages. We learned through trial and error; in the past we followed, we merely reacted. We shriveled in the shadow of another to whom we deferred the authority to choose for us. We gave away the keys to our destiny. We didn't know what to think or to do, and narrowed down our choices so that we didn't have to make any decisions. Our lives got easier and we got numb. Dependent, we shied away from our own power to build a unique experience. We sat in victim energy every time we felt frustrated and disempowered; life happened to us but we didn't seem to happen to it much. We manifested somebody else's magic.

We stumbled but got back on our feet. We tutored ourselves through the industrial and technological revolutions. We are still digesting our recent progression and are learning how to use our new tools as they outgrow and reconfigure themselves incessantly. As we watch the wizardry of global development unfold under our eyes, we feel part of it and we acknowledge our ability to steer our own fate.

Freedom through creativity:

Like the Ram, emblem of the Aries constellation representing the first sign of the zodiac in western astrology and taking its traits from Mars, the god of war and dynamism, we have the capacity to burst open the doors of change with raw energy. As we make millions of mostly unconscious decisions throughout the day, we alter our perception and our environment. We can train to become increasingly aware of our release of creative energy. As we create more consciously, we witness the beneficial changes on our psyche. We unleash our potential and we liberate ourselves through these portals of creativity.

Creativity is in high demand:

Every creation is a first, otherwise it wouldn't qualify as a creation. It is one-of-a-kind by definition. It is unique. What is unique is rare. What is rare is of beauty and fascinates us. Accessing rareness makes us feel beautiful and worthy. The lesser the supply, the higher the demand. What is rare is in high demand.

Our faculty to create is precious and our creativity is in high demand. So it is that we are solicited to deliver our creativity to the world. There is purity and magic in this intention.

The magician within:

The Magician in the mystical Tarot deck is major arcanum number one. The Magician symbolizes the epitome of creativity, embodying our ability to manifest our intentions with higher wisdom. With four principal tools available—skills, materials, ideas, and emotions—in the form of the four suits—wands, pentacles, swords, and cups—the Magician from the Tarot confidently brings higher wisdom down to a practical level.[7] We want to claim our untapped potential. We nurture and express the superhero within. There is an idiot savant extraordinaire in every human being.

We create our reality:

"In the beginning was the Word, and the Word was with God, and the Word was God."[8]

The word is our metaphor for intent. Thought comes first, before it becomes flesh. Plato refers to ideas as non-material abstract forms that possess a higher reality (constant and true) than material physical forms of the World of Forms that are impermanent and therefore unreliable (changeable and deceptive).[9] A thought is a form of intelligence; it is a thread of light intensified with human desire. I create what I look at. I give life where I choose to lay my eyes. I grant my reality to what I see and acknowledge. I birth what I consider.

Tunnel vision is another word for focus:

In being fully engaged, in bringing intensity in our intentions, we will things into existence. Focus is a powerful creation tool. If the laws of nature are fixed, the laws of our perception are flexible and give us endless room to create.

Being creative is paying attention. The more aware we are, the more information we capture and the more stimulation is offered to associate things that have not been combined yet, engendering newness. The world suffers from attention deficit disorder; the fire of focus melts our creative components and then molds them into physical shapes.

Many techniques can enhance focus. Meditation, by helping us to relax and slow down our racing minds, lets us zero in on each thought that pops up. I am interested in creating an online space where we can interact with our creativity privately and at any time, to watch it evolve and monitor our creative progress.

We fragment ourselves in keeping our work life apart:

Many people have a full life of creative and spiritual activities with their friends and family, but they keep them separate from work. This is nothing new. Abraham Lincoln[10] supposedly said, "My father taught me to work, but not to love it. I never did like to work, and I don't deny it. I'd rather read, tell stories, crack jokes, talk, laugh—anything but work." Many of us sympathize with this. Some workers have thrown in the towel and live through their entire work life looking forward to their vacation, without ever hoping for better job days or trying to make their time at work more pleasurable. Creative activities are close to our heart. We cherish them and don't want to reveal, contaminate, or degrade them with our other life, the corporate one of reason, boredom, or hardship. We lock our job life behind closed doors, and we make compartmentalization a norm. Maybe it makes us more focused and more efficient. But it can also make us resigned to the fact that work is an annoyance. We drag our feet to what ends up consuming a third of our days. If we were to bring more of our creativity into our work lives, we would feel less schizophrenic and more accomplished. We would reconcile with our original self, make our business experiences livelier, and bring our teams together. Work would be play. Eventually, creativity can become the makeover factor for work in a corporate environment and improve its dull reputation. We now have to face an even bigger issue: the relationship between corporation and worker has become adversarial. Workers are waking up to the fact that they are not recompensed for the corporate profit they generate with their labor.

Corporate needs a makeover:

As of late creative workers are jumping ship as they see their efforts feeding the corporate machine's insatiable appetite for profit, rather than their own personal welfare. It is understandable that a manager's compensation should be prorated to her/his level of responsibility, but not to the unrestrained extent it has reached today. In 1965 executives earned twenty times more than workers; that number has jumped in 2013 to almost 300 times.[11] The disparity in lifestyles and everyday concerns has estranged bottom and top members of the same organizations to the point where they have no affinity for interacting with one another. In the age of personal empowerment, crowds won't support this increasing salary divide for long. This situation is not viable.

New business models through the respectful use of human resources:

Workers' creativity and productivity are at the center of the debate. In an ideal world, creativity flows both ways from creator to user, from employer to employee. A balanced exchange entails that employees get properly rewarded for their efforts. This is hardly the case today in the corporate configuration. Why should an employee donate her own special ideas to a company that doesn't offer true advantages, such as shared ownership, matching financial bonuses, recognition, and station? When institutions and regulations don't serve our creativity, we take things into our own hands. Wary of being exploited, and at the same time inspired by the success of those empire-building entrepreneurs at the origin of corporations, we search for independent ways to utilize our creative energy to our own benefit. We contemplate joining smaller structures where our voices can be heard, or we even contemplate becoming our own bosses, as we will discuss in chapter 10.

A wake-up call is resounding for big business, with creative minds deserting these systems as this realization snowballs within the collective psyche. The corporate hand will be forced to share wealth if it wants to maintain its presence on the market. We will address this point in chapter 4.

Corporate mechanisms slow down creative emancipation:

The race for profit stifles creativity. Many of my retail clients and corporate workers are not creatively fulfilled in their professions. I heard every day how frustrated designers were, as they had to dilute their creative input in order to sell products to a mass market. At the executive level, creative choices are too often determined by last year's numbers. When decision-makers are financiers, the primary goal is often to generate quick profits to satisfy shareholders and grow their portfolios. When they have the final say on design, they opt to play it safe in the context of a challenging economy by pushing basics that sold well in the past. As a result, the merchandise in-store lacks luster and stays on the shelf, leaving companies stuck with large inventories. Creative products can be a hit or miss in sales; buyers stick to conservative choices and most retailers shy away from risking innovation. They passively wait for global culture to make its way through consumers' psyche until creative products are in higher demand. This could take eons in a cultural media climate that feeds on superficiality.

Sacrificing culture to fast money:

To obtain a more ethical society, consumers have to be educated about ethical consumption. No one is undertaking the huge task to educate them. It costs corporations less brainpower and money to actually keep consumers ignorant and sell them the same stuff over and over again. But the middle executives and workers, who are waking up to the power to put pressure on their directors, realize that they don't know how to educate the masses on better products because they themselves lack proper education.

The value of creativity within the corporate environment:

Creative professionals complain about the challenge to pass new ideas up the chain of command: Staff managers don't speak their cultural language. In a bad economy, budgets for continuing education are cut and only a handful of employees are allowed to travel to the globe's hot spots, where innovation takes place. But also, and more generally, everyone stays put in their field of expertise and receives the education that is conventionally up their alley: It is the logical thing for designers to visit new stores, art shows, and hotels. IT developers attend seminars on start-ups; marketing and finance executives attend the Fortune 500 lectures; finally, production stays home and watches TED Talks. Only a few companies with extra cash to spend send their designers to digital conventions or their CFOs to trend forecasting seminars. When there is no extra budget, cross-disciplinary education is a good bet. It will certainly become more popular as we realize that our creativity sparks when we stand in unknown territory, where all we can do is listen, learn, and even un-learn the old ways. There is great stimulation in being budged out of one's hinges, as in the oyster and grain of sand analogy, or more radically, as in the legend of Scheherazade, who wouldn't have imagined those one thousand and one tales if her life wasn't on the line. But why suffer? Becoming more creative should be uplifting and a common law.

The absence of creativity in our jobs and of fruitful collaboration with our teams are affecting many of us on a personal and social level. Yet creativity is out there. A living entity propelled by an irrevocable force of expansion, it yearns to be expressed, and it needs outlets.

Creative CVs:

At work, a large portion of workers' creative resources remains untapped. It is up to an individual to lay out what he or she wants the world to know. We can revise our curriculum vitae and offer our most special talents to potential employers, those qualities we would want to apply in our dream work life. If we want it, we must say so!

Companies need to know their employees better:

Most of us are hired to perform tasks based on our prior professional expertise or on our educational background, but this practice fails to put to use all of our competencies. During interviews, employers specifically will ask a hypothetical employee about qualifications *they* think can be useful to the company. It's not always appropriate for the worker to share her hobbies or passions unless she's invited to.

Yet the implementation of some of these competencies could inspire new developments and generate solutions for actual or future problems. Throughout our careers, additional information about our personal treasures can reach the ears of our coworkers, but the association of ideas that lead to the utilization of our hidden talents is not always established. Businesses will benefit from broadening their questionnaire during interviews and keeping track of each person's skills.

Adapting to a fast-evolving work force:

People change; they develop new interests that tend to match their true passion more closely as they grow. Businesses will benefit from following their employees' evolution and offering them the opportunity to redefine their position accordingly. Traditional corporate machines stifled by a sluggish bureaucratic system, where one is assigned a task for life, will have trouble adjusting. Smaller business structures can adapt more easily.

A shift in consciousness at the individual level:

For many people living in poverty, the rope is too tight to make ends meet and there is no space for any concern other than survival. But some of us do have a choice. Moral strength comes with age, means, and a foot in the establishment.

Those with wealth might decide to keep a tighter grip on their corporate assets out of fear of losing their security and stability, especially with the planet's resources getting scarcer. Yet a few privileged insiders with a broader vision realize that we have no choice but to redesign the corporate structure into a tool of service to a community larger than just a single percentage of the world's population. Those of us who live in reasonably comfortable conditions have an opportunity to tame our fears and reassess. We can be bold, seize the day, turn our life around, and encourage others to follow.

Change starts with the creativity of each member of society:

In taming our insecurities, we implement change within ourselves. This is the first step to a better society. It is a slow solution, but it works in the long run; we have much to gain from it personally.

We are here to express what we've got and inspire others in turn. When we unleash our creativity, we radiate positive energy and we modify our emotional composition. Our enthusiasm ripples onto our neighbor's energy field. The workplace can change through the creative contribution of employees regardless of their position within the company. So can society, from the inside out, one person at a time.

Becoming an undivided being through creativity:

We already chose creativity at a subliminal level, because creating is our raison d'être. The validity of our existence lies in our creative drive, but we forget the full spectrum of our potential.

When we reconcile with the genuine nature within, we can share with the world the fullest expression of our unique self, which is ultimately connected to a larger dimension of the universe that we have been missing for most of our lives. We can reconcile with the *one*, non-reducible and indivisible creatures that we each truly are: per definition, *individuals*.

This material explores a set of values to engage the user in a sort of questionnaire. It proposes a set of personality archetypes matching each value, prompting each person to identify with these archetypes in a proportion that is unique to their profile.

We like questionnaires; they give us license to spend time with ourselves. When caught up in the formalities of daily life, we forget all the fun things we know and like or are curious about; we abandon our dreams and we sacrifice our passions. This project allows us to recover all facets of our rich personality. It intends to reconcile us with the dynamic and passionate beings that we truly are.

It is the engine we need in our Hall of POWER.

This is an ACT.

The first set of values validates the individuality of the user. It calls for a tool to create a profile unique to each user's *elements*, that is, his or her skills, assets, services, and ideas.

Focused, dynamic, an initiator who stands his ground, the psychological archetype matching this part of our personality is THE PIONEER.

2

HAVE

Owning the Nature of Our Creativity

Resources, Geometry, Metaphysics

Time to break personal rules:

I love the city and its promise of glory. All of us urbanites jump aboard the city wheel to try our good fortune. In tacit agreement, we get busy solving problems, seeking affluence and influence. Sometimes, we experience great fun and cultural stimulation. Some other times, we run errands all day to make another richer, to earn the right to make a living: or so we tell ourselves. The spin on the wheel is such that our primary focus is to stay on. There is little grip to pull ourselves back to the center, to the eye of the storm, to question why we have to work at proving our legitimacy, or whether this really is the lifestyle we prefer and are built for. It is up to us to decide where we fit best; doing so-so in our old styles until we wane and wilt, or brightening up our creative selves. Most of us without personal wealth fear leaving our safe routines behind. We must trust that personal success will ensue.

The benefits of rural life, a break away from maddening waves:

After I left my job I moved to the countryside. I learned how to hear myself think in the over-stimulating buzz of the city. But I needed a quiet place to unclutter my perception.

For some reason, age maybe, or increased sensitivity due to regular meditation, I feel uncomfortable in the presence of vibrations and electric waves from plugged-in appliances and devices. They impair my concentration level, as if my thoughts were short-circuited; my judgment feels clouded. I am certainly not the only one in this position; some folks complain about dizziness around high-voltage power lines, and research institutes recommend caution about exposure to electromagnetic frequencies,[12] even if the risk is said to be minimal as we lack scientific evidence. Mobile phone radiation could have a damaging effect on human health.[13] My house is on top of a hill with a view miles and miles to the south, toward the city. Perched up here, I have a broad perspective on past tribulations and open futures. I pause for a moment. I can plug back into the wired life of the city when I feel up to running the race in excitement. Or I can choose to sit in silence and let the magic of the surroundings take care of me.

Nature's constitution:

Maintaining the land is a commitment. Each season in the country carries its challenges; leaves and wind in the fall, ice and brutal winter cold, melting snows and spring rains, green invasion in the summer. I don't call the shots; for an impatient city girl used to be in charge, surrendering to the pace and will of nature is humbling. I ask to be integrated into the harmony of the whole. My neighbors are deer, fox, wasp, and crow; thorns, dandelion, poison ivy, and garlic mustard. They remind me every day that land, in truth, is a co-op. I must know my place. I am to be a fair guardian to the spirit of these species, and my freedom stops where theirs starts. Or the other way around; sometimes a queen needs to put her foot down.

Asking the essential questions:

I feel blessed to now be able to take time and money out of the equation. Less pressured to produce, I calm the mind chatter and learn to listen to inspiration. I follow in the tracks of wise ones who spend time outdoors to heal and enhance their awareness of life. Here, there is no one to ask me who I am. The question of what I do for a living is irrelevant.

I start over and ask: How can I be of service, what is my fullest expression, who am I to interact with?

Candor is a path to depth:

I connect deeper within, reclaiming the mental space to ask *why* endlessly and unearth what rings true to me. Asking about causal chains that lead to an event is a game that a young child likes to play, until the adult is worn out of answers. Theoretical physicist Brian Greene[14] speaks of his three-year-old son who, while being told a bedtime story about aliens traveling at the speed of light, asks, "Speed of light? What about the speed of dark?" How profound. Children can be existentialist philosophers dressed in the outfit of candor. They surprise us with their genuineness, and when they cannot make sense of our reasons, they question our jurisdiction. They corner us in our incoherencies. Why? What caused this? What caused the cause? The inner child helps us to retrace our own steps back to Source,[15] where unity and perfection reigns. In other words, where things work out.

Naivety as a reevaluation tool:

Time and space must be made in a business environment, even sparsely, for team members to ask these questions, at any executive level of the corporate hierarchy. There are anodyne questions that one without knowledge will ask that can puzzle the expert and help him to reevaluate his belief system. The "child" is not the one it seems. High-ranking professionals can ask about the assembly line operation details, and blue-collar workers can wonder about the brand's strategy, all questions that can eventually lead to the betterment of the company's ways. Naivety works because it is unthreatening. A sheep in wolf's clothing, it breaks defense mechanisms. For decision- makers, there are no silly questions. They will reap benefits from opening up the brand's floor to questions from all boards.

Nature to reconnect with the self:

We have all experienced how quickly we are prone to forget about creative ideas and resolutions imagined while on vacation when coming back to our home and work standards. The reality check is often brutal, as we get thrown back to the same old ways of behaving upon our return, all to keep the ball of corporate financial gains rolling. New ideas generated while away barely stand a chance of being heard.

It seems obvious to advise city-working teams to travel out to the wilderness to hold creative sessions. It is worth making the point again nevertheless: the time spent to travel to a quiet place in nature will be largely compensated by the fluidity with which intellectual juices will flow as a result. Retreats and frequent small breaks in our work lives recharge us and give the chance for progressive ideas gained in relaxed states to be retained.

Reconnecting with our intrinsic nature:

Reconnecting with nature reminds us how every commodity comes about in our life. Access to fresh water is a right that nations lack and fight over. Clean air and unpolluted soil threaten to become luxuries. We are oblivious to the load of labor and time involved in the processes of harvest, manufacturing, and distribution. We take our bread, our shirts, and our smart devices for granted. Money works like magic as we snap our gold fingers and stuff appears. But we fool ourselves into believing that we can live off this trick forever. We can't eat coin. Prestidigitation is not magic, and our personal, social, and corporate values are off. We need to fix our relationship to our physicality in order to dig out the full extent of our potential.

At the end of the cascade of *whys?* lies a pool of values, available to the knowledgeable, long-term thinking, responsible, cool being that we truly are. Coolness indeed is much needed, especially since our species is sitting in a slowly-but-surely warming climate puddle that will get our mood to its boiling point, creating turmoil on the planet.

Fixing our energy problem:

The difficulty of storing energy from renewable sources has been hindering their progress and credibility and has allowed fossil fuel lobbies to perpetrate the systematic plundering of oil, natural gas, and coal, to the detriment of the environment. Alternative energy researchers are working actively on storing excess power[16] from solar panels and wind turbines to limit waste and provide steady electricity,[17] which will drive down the cost of sun and wind energy. On another front, light-emitting diode electricity is rapidly gaining market shares thanks to its longevity, especially now that we have discovered how to use blue LEDs to create longer-lasting white light.[18]

These facts, aside from being good news for the environment, announce a significant change in the use of resources. They are certainly catalysts for an energy revolution with repercussions for the economic and geopolitical environments, provided that governments allow consumers to use these resources directly and affordably. The use of resources in harmony with the environment empowers the individual financially, psychologically, and ethically.

The four elements are our primary resources:

Venus, ruler of the zodiacal constellation of earthy Taurus, is the goddess of fertility. The empress of soil, she reminds us that in order to create tangibility, there has to be matter to create from. The elements are the base matter upon which we create. I had the idea to start from the ground up and call upon the four physical elements to establish a foundation for our creations upon which to build a bridge to our higher consciousness.

Our global culture is imprinted with the elements poetically, mythically, and scientifically. These building blocks are everywhere. The basic natural elements are mentioned as early as the eighteenth century B.C., in the mythological Babylonian tablets *Enûma Eliš*,[19] with references to the sea, sky, wind, and earth. The notion of classical elements finds its roots with the Pythagorean school when Empedocles (490–430 B.C.) standardized perceived composite bodies at four with earth, air, fire, and water.[20] Plato mentions them a few decades later as *stoicheia*, elements, and around 360 B.C. presents five Platonic solids: tetrahedron, cube, octahedron, icosahedron, and dodecahedron, symbolizing fire, earth, air, water, and ether.[21]

The modern notion of the four elements is based on the four natural states of matter: solid, liquid, gas, and plasma.

A personal psychotropic insight on the elements:

In the course of my research in consciousness-altering, I found documentation about natural substances used by indigenous people to connect the human being to the universe. One of these plants, ayahuasca,[22] is an ingestible Amazonian medicine. It contains dimethyltryptamine, or DMT, a compound naturally synthesized in the human body in small quantities from the amino acid tryptophan. DMT has psychotropic effects on the mind and is known to deliver insights on the interconnectedness of all elements in the universe. Shamans call it The Mother, as *she* enables communication with the spirit of the Earth and synchronization with the larger cosmos.

I experimented four times with ayahuasca. The substance allows for a state of consciousness where the journeyman can ask metaphysical questions and receive clear and immediate answers. These come in the form of thoughts, feelings, and physical sensations from what I would describe as the wisdom within.

I only understood after the fourth session the message held for me as a whole in the consecutiveness of these journeys.

The first journey was most memorable. I had no idea of what to expect; yet I was ready and confident. The ritual is sacred and should be honored as such. I formulated the intent to see darkness. It was a bold request, and I got what I asked for, in the most objective manner. The night was cold. I spent most of the imaginative journey in an underground cave with big knotty roots all around me. I took quick trips at night along dark back alleys filled with human dejections, garbage, and putrefaction, populated with all sorts of creatures, crawling, creeping, squeaking, and screeching. I saw moonlit trenches with men stabbing bleeding demons in close combat. I stood by lines of women in single file on a yin yang sign trail, laughing during the day and crying at night at the desolation created by their husbands, brothers, fathers, and sons. I rushed through the tiny world of carbon atoms turning into diamonds over light years of time travel, to slow down and hover by an immense rocky planet, alive and barely moving, suspended in weight and certitude that she wasn't going anywhere ever; it felt like my own womb. None of this appeared as threatening because it seemed to all be related to my body, born of me in the secret of creation, as if darkness was becoming mine.

The second journey took place on a stormy night with heavy rains, and immersed me in the depths of tumultuous yet serene, deep navy and shallow, twinkling waters, and felt like a lesson in spiritual swimming. There was a lot of crying involved, but from love, not pain.

My third journey started at dusk, and as I watched the sun go down, myriad bright colorful concentric geometric patterns appeared as threads of light talking from the sun to each plant and back. I also saw the sun split into two half-disks that would change color, separating in turn into two full disks and merging back in a single ball. Later at night, I could see a chatty laser show of rays taking place between the stars, while a fuzzy moon explained that she only existed in our perception through the sunlight she reflected.

At the start of my fourth journey, I imagined an oppression in my chest suggesting difficulty in breathing; I say suggesting because at no moment did I fear that I wouldn't be able to breathe. I suffered severe asthma as a child and this experience didn't feel similar in any way. I traced my steps back to my first breath, at the cusp between the original pain of breathing and the non-necessity of it, at this key moment of fracture between the worlds of matter and spirit. The wind was hurling about that night, engaging me in what I recall to be quite a humorous conversation.

I trusted that there had to be a message behind all this, but I wasn't sure which one. I thanked the Mother within for the lesson. This four-step expedition was an orchestration that invited me to an intimate dance with the elemental realm. Earth, water, fire, and air each took their turn and unlocked secrets in relation to what I needed to know.

Later, when I envisioned the creation of a platform that would work as a link between our physical and spiritual realities, between corporations and values, between earth and heaven, between elements and archetypes, I remembered.

The four elements as the foundation to describe our human treasures:

I made the arbitrary decision to pair by analogy the four elements to the possible assets at the disposal of human beings; not only material possessions, but also competences, ideas, and services that we can provide to each other.

This incredible variety of all that we have to offer can be placed into the four following categories:

The element of earth is ascribed to all things we can touch: objects, buildings, money, and so forth.

The element of fire represents all skills, know-how, experience, or expertise.

The element of water represents all services we can perform to help others, such as nursing, teaching, managing, or mediating.

Finally, the element of air represents our intellectual capability for ideas, philosophy, or strategy.

With our spirits' magical wands, we can combine and animate these elements into endless creations.

I intend to use the four elements as a language base for our tool of exchange to categorize all the treasures that users will describe in their profile. With Earth, we have; with Fire, we do; with Water, we care; with Air, we think.

Nature and culture are two complementary pillars of physical reality:

The concept of four elements is both natural and cultural. We can file every occurrence we experience, every opportunity we come into contact with, or every palpable object, into two categories: the innate or the man-made. Every concept can be substantiated in either one slot or in both. Craft or industrialism, tribalism or globalism, tradition or modernism, all lean against the sturdy pillars of nature and culture.

In my former career, I did a project for an American hotel and resort chain to uplift its brand image, which had degraded over the years. I presented eight propositions around the themes of nature and culture. Earthy and artistic, communal and connected, spiritual and futuristic, playful and customer-centric, were the hybrid themes chosen to simplify the strategy yet take into account the complex needs of a multicultural international clientele. This simple classification allowed for clarity. The core values that needed to be brought back to the forefront of the brand's image were redefined. The executive direction was able to select from the various natural and cultural ingredients and make their own brand-appropriate mix to rebuild a unique image. Today, their hotels present a much more pleasant ambience than the superficial, loud club mood that they had turned into.

These two pillars are not mutually exclusive:

Nature and culture don't operate in right/wrong mode. They don't force us to choose one or the other. There is more to them than polarity and Manichaeism. In nature there is instinct, which no physical body can deny; in culture there is intent, which no mind dares denigrate. With these two great teachers on our side, as reminders of what our civilization is about, we bypass the battle between good and bad. We hold the judgment-free blank canvas of our future creations.

Nature and culture see new potentials; they act warmly and are welcoming. Our instincts widen and our intents lengthen on this two-axis plane.

The spirit of geometry:

At the source of nature and culture are patterns; at the source of patterns is geometry.

There is a reason for everything. As far back as we look, there is always a cause. I can't recall the complex series of happenings that kneaded the tree branch in its singular texture, color, and shape. I can't remember the tree's past. I am missing chunks in that chain of events. Randomness, one of the many faces of the unexplained, is amnesia. I lost my memory. What I call random, I call a miracle; I call it sacred, I call it God.

"Plutarch attributed the belief that God created the universe according to a geometric plan to Plato, who said that God geometrizes continually. In modern times the influential eighteenth-century mathematician Carl Friedrich Gauss adapted this quote, saying 'God arithmetizes;'" so quotes the global voice of Wikipedia[23] on sacred geometry.

Harnessing the power of entropy in our home and work environments:

To the human eye, chance is an opportunity to dream. We love what is random. It surprises us and we love to be surprised. We can just sit in front of the tree in innocence, in awe and delight, creating our own story about the branch. Randomness gives our mind a workout, and it invigorates our imagination. It is an engine for creativity. After all, penicillin was discovered by chance by Alexander Fleming in 1928 when he fortuitously left open a Petri dish containing staphylococcus bacteria. By chance, the dish was invaded by the *Penicillium notatum* mold, which killed the bacteria. Instead of discarding the contaminated sample, Fleming studied it.

Science uses the word entropy to describe the degree of disorder in a system. When a system is in a state of complete disorder, it is in chaos; chance rules.

In the context of our lives, leaving room for chaos can bring astounding benefits. It leads one to profound behavioral changes. It entices coworkers to accept the idea of transformation of a work project or a corporate process. Leaving some time and space for disorder helps teams welcome change.

Geometry is the source of physical reality:

To an all-seeing eye, randomness is a beautiful illusion. If I was shown the collection of all the storms the tree has ever weathered, every sun's ray on its foliage, every photon, every hit the woodpecker tapped onto its trunk, every insect the bird dug out, every child that climbed up the branches, the size, shape, and impact of their heel according to their strength, speed, weight and age, then I could tell the full story of the branch in strings of consecutive and simultaneous patterns. I could recite the branch's complete mathematical formulae.

If we were to recover the memory of who we have come to be, peeling off the layers of time, scrutinizing the full picture that led us to our present shape, we would see a combination of nature and culture, with DNA, lineage, and history intertwined in an intricate network of mathematical laws. Geometry is space, distance, memory; it transcends time. Essence and truth are found at the source of geometry.

Using sacred geometry to design a web platform:

I am curious to see whether designing a web platform according to sacred geometry can have the same appeasing or energizing effect on us. I wish to experiment and apply the golden ratio and Fibonacci sequencing—a recurring natural pattern in biology—in the design aesthetics for the movement of objects or in the programming on the front and back ends of a site.

Geometric patterns do a number on us:

The alignment of patterns has the power to appease, disrupt or energize our senses. Some abstract geometric symbols make us feel safe and balanced.

Geometric beauty is in every nook and cranny of our natural environment. The designs following the golden ratio in a human ear or a nautilus shell, in the arrangement of sunflower seed heads. Pine cones and cauliflower all contain algorithms that can have a subliminal effect on us, as if they were replicating and reflecting the perfection of our cellular alignment and the purity of Source. Frequency and resonance obey geometry. Whether we absorb them through our visual or auditory abilities, contemplating shapes or listening to harmonic sound associations, these stimuli seem to untangle invisible knots and coordinate our energy centers in deeper realms of our being. As if the carbon structure of our biology was turning into a crystalline one, transmuting matter into diamond.

On a broad scale, I wonder how the view of the ocean, mountains, a desert, or a rolling landscape, or the sound of crashing waves, the wind in the foliage or the high-pitched singing of birds, have the power to make our blood pressure drop. All of these things possess a multi-drawer geometry. Maybe we have the cerebral faculty to embrace mathematical complexities when we look at billions of grains of sand. Some instance in our brain might be able to synchronize the myriad of reflecting algorithms in sea waves and understand the interactions between space, matter, and energy at quantum scale. Maybe we can synthesize the full blueprint of such a massive orchestration of perfectly coordinated microcosms, soothing the eye and the mind. Maybe it works wonders on our endocrine regulation, generating secretion of hormones and neurotransmitters that dope us into beatitude.

Man-made geometry to design a computer tool:

The sight of geometric patterns in art or architecture captivates me. I feel as if an alignment takes place in an inner chamber of my understanding of reality, and I am able to relate. A building such as the Taj Mahal, patterns of Islamic mosaics, artwork and drawings by M.C. Escher,[24] or fractals unfurling on the screensavers of our computers are designed in proportions and motions that can hypnotize us into a feeling of wellness.

Metaphysics as a bridge from spiritual values to business:

I truly enjoyed the grounding character of the humane discipline of metaphysics and its solid connection to man's physical experience. The Stoic thinker Epictetus declares: "Philosophy does not claim to secure anything for us outside our control. Otherwise it would be taking on matters that do not concern it. For as wood is the material for the carpenter, and marble that of the sculptor, so the subject matter of the art of life is the life of the self."[25]

Philosophy, the love of wisdom, is a way of life that deals with the nature of things and their cultural connotations. So does metaphysics, the branch of philosophy explaining what is after, or beyond—depending on the school of interpretation[26]—the study of physics. What makes metaphysics so appealing is that it reconciles the immutability of the laws of nature with the changeability of our perception of them. The purpose of metaphysics, or ontology, the study of the fundamental nature of being, is to establish a bridge between the tangible and the intangible, of which spirituality can be considered a part.

The language of metaphysics is rather abstract, sometimes poetic. Abstraction leaves a margin for interpretation. A philosophical approach makes space for beauty in our inner dialogues, and for openness in our team discussions. It gives us room to breathe our creations. It is our new best friend that will help us reinvent our business ethics.

Ancient wisdom traditions, belief systems, and the teachings of mystery schools carry similar messages:

For years, I have gathered information about the myths behind celestial objects, our chakra centers and ancient medicine principles, alchemy, various techniques of numerology, religious texts, occultism, and sacred symbols.

At the source of these teachings, preceding the many colorful and sometimes far-fetched human interpretations, *we find common values* independent from their provenance. I searched for ethics that would be amenable to many schools of thought, to initiate a conversation on spirit and matter. Layering these teachings, I searched for a point of congruence at which the various meanings click into place like levers in a lock. At this confluence, each layer releases information that can be decrypted and enriched by the layer of the neighboring tradition, and remains open like a sluice to allow our intelligence to flow from higher consciousness to physical reality and apply this wisdom to our mundane life.

The best of all possible worlds, or the search for common denominators:

Mathematician and philosopher Gottfried Wilhelm Leibniz looks for "the best of all possible worlds" in his *Theodicy: Essays on the Goodness of God, the Freedom of Man, and the Origin of Evil,* published in 1710. Leibniz wrote after studying metaphysical commonalities between Eastern and Western philosophies or various Christian ecumenical traditions. Mocked by French Enlightenment philosopher Voltaire in *Candide, ou l'Optimism* (first published in 1759) and portrayed as a happy fellow unaware of the harsh reality of human life, Leibniz's

31

precepts lost favor among the European intelligentsia, especially after the great Lisbon earthquake of 1755, a catalyst for Voltaire to write *Candide*.

However, Einstein's more recent theory of relativity brought back a scientific interest in the concept of the cohesion of matter, and by extension a philosophical interest in pantheism. The more recent development of computer technology, largely based on Leibniz's *Explanation of Binary Arithmetics,* also contributed to a rediscovery of the German philosopher, who was a Sinophile and took inspiration from the 0–1 binary I Ching system for his discovery of the calculus, the mathematics of movement and change based on infinitesimality and continuity to define derivatives and integrals.

With the theory of the "best of all possible worlds," Leibniz proposed mathematical and philosophical common denominators and related them to human life. We can appreciate this concept once we bypass the author's religiosity, the topic of which will be discussed in chapter 9. He reminded us that a harmonious tango is possible between the loops of unity (zeros) and the lines of uniqueness (ones), two major components of today's binary computer language. Leibniz offered his mathematical contribution to the search for common denominators between metaphysics and technology, a bridge essential to this book on values from spirit to business.

The validity of a metaphysical language for the work environment:

A communication system bridging unity and duality will allow us to recover a way to function that is in agreement with our biological and social environments.

The business world is in critical need of ethics. Shifting consciousness in the upper layers of the business world is a tough call. Most of those at the top are too comfortable to change their position. Yet the shifting process is already engaged. We must rely on the emulative power of enthusiastic folks who come together to discuss innovative solutions and convince reluctant superiors to alter their strategies, lest they see their smartest elements take their creativity to greener pastures. Visionary executives and workers desiring to engage in a new conversation on bringing values to the business world will find beneficial a philosophical language that, despite its apparent complexity, can bring more humanity to our process of reevaluation and can improve our work ways. I believe that the discipline of metaphysics can help us to find common denominators and facilitate our progress.

This project uses nature and culture as a foundation for the setup of our fundamental values, under the supervision of philosophy and metaphysics.

It calls for geometry and elements as building blocks to describe our desires and manifest our creations.

It is the prime matter we need in our Hall of FABRICATION.

This is a RESOURCE.

The second set of values calls for a tool to describe the identity of the user, of an organization, of a project.

This tool is a description application; it offers twelve categories (the twelve values) where the attributes inherent to a project, an organization, or the self can be organized in the form of words.

It is a sorting tool to enter all data (market research, notes, etc.) perceived by the user and file them by value. It helps to confirm one's intuition, or "hunches" about global currents and consumers' attitudes.

In the future and upon funding, the capability for a larger memory to store and process visuals, sounds, videos, etc. will be added.

Descriptive, laborious, handy, the psychological archetype matching this part of our personality is THE ARTISAN.

2.5

SURRENDERING TO THE MAGIC OF CREATION

The threshold for emotional release:

At that turning point when boiling water turns into steam, there is an explosion; freezing water fissures the toughest rocks. Shamans plan ceremonies at dusk or at dawn, when light meets dark, at locations where the sea meets the earth or the forest meets the meadow, for it is at the edge of landscapes, at the cusp of opportunities, at the brink of becoming, in the space between things, in the cracks of discontinuity, that the spirit world opens its secrets and wonders occur.

Change is an agent of creation:

There is power right at the door between the quiet safety of home and the crude noisy world beyond it. When we go to sleep, we can train to balance on the fence between a dream and a waking state, between physicality and other planes of existence. In this intermediary state we can transport ourselves wherever we want while maintaining the same lucidity as the one we are used to in physical reality. With perseverance and training, we can induce alternate states of perception of our own choosing, as scientifically described in the works of American researcher Robert Monroe in the 1950s on astral projections.[27]

When we linger in the unstable space of the undone, when we face incompatibility, we grant ourselves the privilege to access future manifestations. There is an opportunity to create every time we stand fearless in front of a challenging task, every time we hold steady between team workers who have little in common yet must work together. Creation is in gestation in the anticipation of change.

The sinkhole of creation, a creed for newness:

There is a sinkhole between our creative desire and its manifestation. Right at that instant, right before we follow through with our intentions, there is a micro-realm filled with intense potential. We poise within the blink where creation simmers. *Stasis,* the state of being static, is a launch pad for creations-to-be. Like the archer with a pulled bow, we stand aiming in great anticipation of the release of future manifestation.

Did we really think that the hollow space between objects was empty? It is anything but. Science used to advocate this. But when it calculated that intergalactic space had a mass, it changed its mind to define the void in the universe as dark matter and a living organism called *spacetime*[28] *singularity.*[29] New stars are brought to life[30] in the wombs of black holes.

It is interesting to note that a Google search for synonyms defines the word *singular* as the following: *remarkable, extraordinary, exceptional, outstanding notable, noteworthy*, and as the Oxford dictionary states, *denoting or referring to just one person or thing*. The very definition of creation.

Ancient traditions combine magic with knowledge, communication and humor:

The mystical tradition of the Jewish Kabbalah calls this enigmatic instance of our consciousness *Da'at,*[31] Hebrew for *knowledge*. On the Tree of Life,[32] it represents the etheric state of unity where all other instances converge within the self. This point is not always depicted on diagrams representing the Tree of Life, because it is hidden from the perspective of physical reality, and it stands for the mystery element.

The Tree of Life mirrors the human body and interestingly locates Da'at at the level of our throat, which is also the seat of our chakra of communication.

Communication is the attribute of Hermes the messenger, the zodiac icon of the Gemini constellation, which is also the *third* sign in

Western astrology, and the chapter number we are about to approach here. The energy of the Gemini is paired with that of the joker; he puts on his mask of laughter or tears and becomes its twin. Both Dr. Jekyll and Mr. Hyde, he plays the card of his own *Doppelgänger*. To the Native American Lakota people the coyote is the symbol for *Heyoka*,[33] the teacher of wisdom through trickery. The trickster is a great magician, making us trip through the traps of our own paradoxes and transform a situation through laughter and surprise.

Humor is a master teacher in creativity:

If there is one creative therapy that deserves a medal, it is laughter. The comedic aspect in situations and words is the most efficient reconciler, and its facets are endless. One can play at will with this amazing teacher that is accepted everywhere like a global and free currency. Laughter is a lapse of joy suspended in space; it takes off all edges and disarms hostility. A laughing team is more inclined to compromise and accept new ideas. Humor is creation and facilitates more of it. I actually believe that laughing sessions should be mandatory at home and at work. A day without laughing is indeed a lost day.

All these elements from diverse cultures concur to speak of the big mystery of humanity, the mystery of creation. In the nothingness we become of form.

This chapter falls into the blank between the magic of unity and the nature of duality.

In this vacuum, traditions click into place to reveal chapter *3* on mediation, messengers and alchemy, giving us access to our third dimension, and allowing for the manifestation to take shape in front of our eyes.

This is A WELL.

3

MEDIATE

Bridging Our Creativity with Our Soul

Alchemy, Missing Link, Messenger

The depth of creation:

Our bodily experience is three-dimensional. Earthy creations live in length, width, and depth. Our eyes, apart from each other, allow us to see with two different angles to give perspective to the world. An object seen through one eye only exists in two dimensions and appears as flat; it doesn't hold the distance. An idea understood from one side only will be given substance when apprehended by a second opinion, and even more by a third. The more perspectives a concept can hold, the deeper its scope. A weak product satisfies only one consumer requirement, such as a food product that has a satisfactory taste but no nutritional value. A decent food product has taste and nutrition. A great food product has taste, nutrition, and is produced in environmentally sustainable conditions and labor ethics.

The system of values we are exploring through this material proposes twelve dimensions to check on the validity of a product, a concept or the identity of a person or an organization. Once all these layers are explored and their requirements matched, the depth of the concept is validated; a long and successful life lies ahead. The more dimensions, the closer the fit to one's desire. It is up to anyone to choose at which depth level they want to position their projects. Creators of a start-up offering entertainment functions but no information will build quick profit and rush to sell their business before consumers get tired of it. A start-up with function, information, and educational resources has longevity; it can even become a model for other enterprises.

Our internet experience is two-dimensional; I am interested in building an online tool with a perspective that delivers depth.

Accessing our depth:

Depth speaks volume; it is the life-giving agent of earthly manifestation. Depth is the plus that changes everything. To create we must go to our depths. Depth is found in truth. Our human depth is of a spiritual nature.

An elixir of human ascension:

Alchemy is a metaphysical recipe to help the individual transcend to a higher level of consciousness. It shows the path toward transmuting earthy lead into spiritual gold. It is the added value that dusts off our flat two-dimensional basics and turns them into multifaceted shimmering riches.

Alchemy has the power to turn corruption, disease, and mortality into incorruptibility, health, and immortality. Alchemy knows a universal elixir to help man remember its divinity, its royal blood; *sang real* in Old French, an expression that once contracted gave the name to the word *Graal*, or grail.

Alchemy, an Hermetic tradition:

This Medieval and Renaissance protoscience is the precursor to chemistry. It is concerned with the composition of substances; Robert Boyle (1627–1691), who started his research in the tradition of alchemy, is considered the father of modern chemistry[34] because of his experimental research on the pressure of gas.

Alchemy is linked to Hermeticism, the dual worship of the Greek messenger Hermes and of Thoth, the Egyptian deity of knowledge, wisdom, and hieroglyphs. The two entities were merged in late antiquity into a binary god called Hermes Trismegistus, or "Thrice-Great" in Greek; its wisdom sits on the three disciplines of alchemy, astrology, and theurgy, the practice of rituals.

According to the *Encyclopaedia Brittanica*, alchemy teachings grew arcane when "the art degenerated into a mass of superstition." They fell from grace as the word *hermetic* became synonymous with *occult*. Quite the etymological irony, since Hermeticism derives its name from Hermes, the god of communication. The *Encyclopaedia* reflects conventional disbelief in scholarly circles on this topic; adepts of alchemy throughout the ages have kept their research away from inquisitive eyes all too ready to label them as heretics or fools. Scientists of reputation have dabbled with the practice. Isaac Newton had a keen lifetime interest in occultism and spent twenty years researching the philosopher's stone. According to his biographer Robert Skidelsky, economist John Maynard Keynes led a "coded life with much of the essential hidden from prying eyes." This instinct for privacy extended to the belief that "beneath the knowledge in which he publicly dealt there lay an esoteric knowledge open only to a few initiates."[35] He purchased Newton's alchemical papers in 1942, and wrote: "Newton was not the first of the age of reason, he was the last of the magicians, the last of the Babylonians and Sumerians, the last great man which looked out on the visible and intellectual world with the same eyes as those who began to build our intellectual inheritance rather less than 10,000 years ago."[36]

Today's mind is freer from the limits of dogma and is interested in reenacting past teachings. Alchemy is a tradition available to anyone interested in spiritual transformation, and has always been. The twelve alchemical processes can be translated in many languages. These processes are: calcination, congelation, fixation, dissolution, digestion, distillation, sublimation, separation, incineration, fermentation, multiplication, and projection.[37] I regularly work on verbal and visual interpretations of these concepts for practical applications in various business domains. They can inspire treatments or finishes for design products and their transformative actions can translate into strategies in the fields of communication, banking, hospitality, or entertainment.

Alchemy as a messenger to wisdom:

When people seek spiritual answers, alchemy resurfaces in the global mind. This is the case today, in our times of liberty of expression, as there exists a renewed interest in matters of ancient culture, philosophy, and spirituality among a community of empowered individuals who want to take an active part in the ascension of humanity. Actually, if society can be transmuted one individual at a time, the sole intention of betterment of the self makes one an alchemist. Our project has an alchemical property when its goal is met to help individuals deepen their values and improve their life experience through creativity.

The three alchemical principles:

Alchemy offers transcendence from basics to an elevated sense of completeness, from dullness to beauty, from material to immaterial.

It operates through three philosophical principles that rule our bodies, our minds, and our emotional states, but also rule planets, plants, minerals, and animals. These three principles are sulfur, mercury, and salt. Occultist Arthur Edward Waite (1857–1942) writes: "*Sulphur* signifies Nature, and *Mercury* the supernatural. The inseparable connection of the two in man is called *Sol,* but as these three are seen to be indissolubly one, the terms may be used interchangeably."[38]

Sulfur is the fiery, radiating, diffusive principle, relating to the human soul, the essence of the human being. Mercury is the fluid, dissolving, mediating principle, relating to the human spirit. Salt is the contracted, crystallized principle, relating to the human body.

The three modalities in Western astrology:

Astrology also operates according to three modalities by which the twelve zodiac entities interact with each other. The cardinal modality initiates a situation, the fixed modality maintains a situation, and the mutable modality allows for the transformation of a situation. The astrological categories called houses relate to these qualities and display the modes of expression of action, security, and learning; they are described respectively as Angular, Succedent, and Cadent.[39]

A tripartite system recognized globally for millennia:

Symbols in many traditions reflect this tridimensional axis of active principles. In the Hindu traditional medicine of Ayurveda, three bodily humors called doshas circulate through our physiology: vata, pitta, and kapha make up the human body's constitution, governing physiological activity. The ancient Chinese manual of divination *I Ching,* or Book of Changes, uses trigrams and hexagrams derived from triangular combinations of the Tao's yin and yang polarities.

The Celtic triskelion used in the European Iron Age presents three interlocked spirals symbolic of a non-dualistic cosmology. The Japanese mitsudomoe at the foundation of the Shinto religion represents union of man, earth, and sky.[40] The *Gakyil* or Wheel of Joy[41] is a symbol of perfection for Tibetan Buddhism and indivisibility between the Base, the Path, and the Fruit. Christian traditions present the trinity of the Father, Son, and Holy Spirit with the triquetra, a trefoil knot illustrating various religious manuscripts and used on metalwork.

These teachings have in common the three-dimensional representation of the interwoven dynamics between everything that exists and allows humanity to ascend into greatness. They certainly remind us of the nuclear trilogy formed by the electron, the proton, and the neutron with their negative, positive, and neutral electric charges.

The added value of a three-dimensional program:

This triple system of principles invokes metaphors, symbols, myths, and legends to describe both material life and the energies that move our spirits. It speaks to scientists, to philosophers, to artists. It builds paths of understanding where unlikely bedfellows can communicate to co-weave elements in new associations.

It establishes bridges between the physical and the ethereal worlds. It describes reactions between things, people, and thoughts; it demonstrates fluidity between the animate and the inanimate, shaping a grand unified field[42] within our perception. It adds a *tri*-nary element to our binary world. Triality takes over duality.[43]

Using three active principles to activate our treasures:

A software tool could be built where the user's personal traits and qualities, comprised of material goods, competences, services, and ideas would be described by the four elements and handled in three different manners according to the trilogy of alchemical and astrological principles.

They would be brought to life by the power of these verbs, describing the processes of initiating, maintaining, or transforming actions.

The third element is the missing link:

Polarity is second nature to humanity. We are familiar with our binary axes of good and evil, of reason against emotion, of gender attraction between male and female, of zeros and ones, of alternating current, etc. Yet there is always a third element, located in between polarities. Its presence is muted, neutral, and strange.

This third element is silent and filled with promises, like an apostrophe, like the brief letter *Yod* present in many Semitic languages, and it associated with the symbol of the Immaculate Conception[44] in the Kabbalah Tree of Life. A *Yod* figure in astrology is a triangular pattern linking two planets at a balanced angle to each other, to a third planet that has no commonality of gender, cardinality, or elementarity with either one of the first two. In an astrological chart, this configuration is considered disruptive yet filled with the potential to evolve after fated confrontation with our shortcomings. It is called the Finger of God,[45] understandably so.

The forgotten third:

The sleeping *third* is the equation of human life. The Kabbalistic Tree of Life presents three pathways of consciousness. The Pillar of Severity on the left and the Pillar of Mercy on the right each hold only three progressive instances of perception, or Sephirots, that are vertically aligned. The middle pillar of Moderation reaches all the way from the top to the bottom through five Sephirots, allowing circulation on the Tree between Kether at the top (divine unity) and Malkuth at the bottom (physical reality).[46] As Tibetan Buddhism also recognizes, the Middle Way to a better life is found along the central path of moderation, not within polarities.

We have dismissed this dormant particle, because we didn't understand its role. Caught on our fast-spinning wheel, we have neglected the capital importance of this "time-out" moment. Or maybe we have silenced it because its mystery scares us.

Yet the world is changing; our minds and hearts are opening up.

Braving our limits:

The exponential increase in scientific discoveries and the limitless and instant access to information are signs of this expansion. So are the nanosecond flash trading of financial funds or the self-confidence of individuals to foment political rebellions at the grassroots level, and the resulting high demand for transparency in all sectors of the public domain.

We are psychologically ready to take on more. We seek intensity. We are becoming more curious about our emotional mechanisms. Graphic snapshots of war, sex, and infamy inundate newsrooms. We feed on reality shows and watch vampire movies at a young age. There is a voyeur and an inquisitive character within us. We are reclaiming our blood. We expose our inner core, and as a result we develop acceptance toward disruption as we separate our identity from our emotion-generated dramas. We realize that our persona is not limited to our feelings.

News spread like gunpowder via lightning-fast media and the intuitive quality of our electronic communication devices. Information is disclosed instantaneously and for all to see, and there is less time or space for official censoring. We are becoming jugglers of data; we endorse the human complexities that we create. We educate our youth about the dangers of cyber malfeasance rather than blocking information, because we realize that parental censorship is losing its grip just as drama is losing its luster. More facts are disclosed, because we welcome the lessons that bring the outdated patterns of right and wrong back to our attention to allow us to release them. We need values to hold down our psychological sanity.

Spirited and spiritual:

Knowledge invites self-confidence and triggers permissiveness. We become more blasé, hence lighter-hearted. We play the tragicomic twin game of Drama versus Humor to bring spirit into our lives. Again, laughter is a powerful healer and a great emotional transformer. It is a mediator to the spirit world. We have made God punitive and serious, while in truth god[47] empathizes and loves a good laugh. We are clearing our collective past; we are ready to transform our experience and transcend to become empowered creators.

Patience is silence in gestation:

In our hurried society, we are *Slaves to the Rhythm*, as Grace Jones sang in the competitive industrial era of the eighties.

Patience is found in the non-doing, the eye of the cyclone, in the midst of neutrality. It is not a burden, but a respite that allows creation to take place.

Nothing ever remains the same, as impermanence is an agent of physical reality. The grace of the global dance of creation has many surprises in store to help us accomplish our heart's desires. We forget to trust that miracles are only waiting for us to let them into existence. We forget that the universe knows better and that patience is a virtue.

In corporate culture, the global tendency to rush and generate short-term gains to please impatient shareholders affects company values. Management revs faster and ever more superficially to generate profits, relegating crucial ethical questions to the end of the to-do list, where they never get tackled.

The creative process won't be hurried. When stressed by impatience, creation comes out incomplete and dysfunctional.

In a creative work session, a rushed solution is often short-lived or mis-fitted.

Creation within the breath:

In the yoga breathing exercises known as *pranayama*, the essence of the divine is to be found between the in-breath and the out-breath; the practice of retention of the breath between inhalation and exhalation is used as a path to enlightenment. *Antar kumbakha*, the state of suspension of breath with filled lungs after full inhalation, stabilizes our perception with a balancing effect before the breath can be let out and redistributed equally between organs. *Baya kumbhaka*, the state of suspension of the breath with empty lungs after full exhalation, allows for temporary detachment from strings of reality and brings clarity.[48] Every single breath is pregnant with the opportunity to create anew.

Creation is the mechanism by which geometry sets and manifestation happens:

This undisclosed third factor piques our curiosity. This missing link is where matter agglomerates, is held in place, and morphs into a new creation. New associations spin, overlap, and merge their geometry fluidly in the realm of potentials, in and out of our temporal reality, until they set in the collective desire. When they do set, fixation occurs. Concrete manifestation has no choice but to take place.

Magic is creation:

The third zodiac sign ends with the summer solstice, a transition from the light-filled airy vibration of the Gemini into the nurturing waters of the Cancer mood. It is the turning point at which our days become warmer, but also shorter. This first inversion of the year, a pirouette into the mysteries of our heart, occurs right here in the energy of the number 3, in the momentum of our intent to create.

Both gods involved in Hermeticism, Hermes and Toth, are associated with magic and writing; alchemy is a messenger of magic. In our desire to simplify our lives, we have numbed ourselves to the wonders of mystery and magic, but they are now resurging and winking at us. Physician, botanist, alchemist, and occultist Paracelsus (1493–1541), states: "Magic has power to experience and fathom things which are inaccessible to human reason. For magic is a great secret wisdom, just as reason is a great public folly."[49]

The number 3 is odd and a carrier of miracles. It gives us the chance to rebuild the severed linkage with our ancient cultures, to reincorporate our spirituality into our incomplete modern day mentality. It reinstates the *non-said third* that is asking for recognition.

The power in synthesis:

This project is a bridge. It is a binding agent that reconnects us with the question marks of our personalities. It allows us to create a synthesis out of the polarity of the thesis and antithesis of our internal discourse. It makes our elements active through three verbs: initiating, maintaining, and transforming. Like the chemicals in the synapse process of our brain, this portal is a necessary vehicle of information; it explains, understands, decodes, and thereby helps us to fine-tune and strengthen the foundation without which our creations cannot be birthed.

This Rosetta Stone is a tie for aspects of an individual's personality. It serves as a mediator between users, groups, and projects. It is a networking tool.

It is the translator we need in our Hall of COMMUNICATION.

This is an INTERVENTION.

The third set of values calls for a matchmaking tool to connect creative of various backgrounds, offering them the missing skills to start their new projects.

Witty, mercurial, and a great interpreter, the psychological archetype matching this part of our personality is THE MESSENGER.

4

GATHER

Embracing Our Creative Impulses

Family, Female, Womb, Collective, Circle

A need for boundaries:

Too many choices paralyze us. An excess of freedom can hurt us if we don't have inner buffers to prevent confusion; there are many political, social, or psychological examples illustrating the challenge of autonomy. It takes many stages to move a country's regime from authoritarianism to democracy. A society without structures can fall prey to feudalism under the sword of abusive warlords. It takes education and acceptance for a people to handle free speech peacefully after years of censorship, or to modify one's sexual behavior from puritanism to hippiedom. When freedom pushes our level of tolerance too far, we break our circuits; we reject new ideas as unsettling and we miss the opportunity to get over our fears and open up. Too much light disintegrates us if we don't have the lightning rod to diffuse the excess jolt of energy. It requires strength to anchor liberty; light and love are powerful forces that one must be prepared to hold in. The voices of creativity all speak at once in our mind; we need a box to catch the precious words of inspiration before they disappear into thin air.

While we acquire more knowledge and expand to incorporate more emotional, social, and spiritual blessings into our being, we need a recipient to retain our learning process.

A cozy nest to go back to when we embark on a mission of self-discovery:

This project offers a repository for all the new ventures that we will want to explore. Its frame is built as a support to prevent us from stumbling under the load, overstretching through diversity, or overheating in passion. When we keep our skills, desires, and potentials in labeled boxes, we contain our raw impulses until we sort out which ones are the most appropriate to experience for the time being, saving some for the devil. We can regroup ideas safely until they are mature enough to evolve into projects.

The grail, a principle of love and reconnection with the self:

Merging of the male and female seeds happens within the female body. Creation needs a matrix. Our creativity seeks a receptacle.

The legend of the Holy Grail finds its origins in the twelfth century in Celtic mythology, medieval Welsh literature, and Christian traditions. Mostly known as the symbol of a sacred quest, the Holy Grail was lost and could only be found by the perfect knight (Parsifal/Percival), allowing the union between the ideal masculine and feminine principles.

The Holy Grail originally refers to fasting, later becoming a representation of nourishment. The chalice is a depiction of the concept of communion, from the blood of Christ nurturing the Christian's spirit at mass, to the nineteenth-century artistic movement Symbolism's interpretation of female blood and fertility.

One of the four suits in the mystical Tarot is the suit of cups. Cups hold feelings; the element of water is their symbol.[50] A sacred grail is a container that welcomes the female and male parts of our soul and allows for the assembling of our emotional puzzle. It is the private space where one picks up the pieces of the psyche and mends holes.

In allowing users to experiment with their creativity, the project helps them to build confidence and a healthy relationship with the self, without which a healthy relationship with others cannot be established.

Business is about people:

Successful companies offer great products and services to consumers. Those products and services sell because they are useful and appealing in and out. A winning combination of purpose and design meets the market's requirements. But the human resource factor is also a vital measurement of achievement: business is about work ethics and happy workers as much as it is about stuff. The tiny country of Bhutan officially evaluates its success at large through the psychological index of Gross National Happiness (GNH),[51] a set of the four pillars of "good governance, sustainable socio-economic development, cultural preservation, and environmental conservation" classified in the nine following domains: "psychological well-being, health, education, time use, cultural diversity and resilience, good governance, community vitality, ecological diversity and resilience, and living standards."

The work environment can benefit from measuring its success, the degree of fulfillment, excitement, and sense of purpose felt by its employees. Creativity is a standard for business achievement, and it is a human factor. Sometimes who we work with and how we work together matters as much as the products we make and how we distribute them. Team binding is a requisite to a brand's success.

We can build work tools that reinforce cohesion between team members, while maintaining the standards of esthetics and purposefulness for products that sell and bring income to generate budgets to feed employees' creativity even further.

Online promotion:

A messaging system inherent to the project can be designed for users to engage with one another to discuss and create collectively. Once a project is solid, it can make its debut into the world. Some ideas will be strong enough to be exposed to a few trusted peers, or to the public.

When we dare to share our creations on the project's network, we might be surprised by the acclamation received from other users or groups whose support can help us carry out our dreams.

Who knows—many wonderful ideas never shine because they are not publicized. Encouragement from the outside world serves as motivation, and social media has become a key tool for independent marketing and self-promotion.

The geo-political landscape of the future:

With the advent of the internet, geographical proximity is no longer required to maintain a tightly knit community. Individuals with common values who are not physical neighbors can now bond online in dispersed formations, just as high-functioning as before.

City-states from antiquity to modern day have been defined by their exclusiveness, independence, and sovereignty over contiguous territory and have served "as centers and leaders of political, economic and cultural life." More and more *community-states* are sprouting today that are just as promising and even more autonomous than city-states; their loose territory is constantly reconfigured by traveling members, or "hypernomads and virtual nomads," to use a term coined by the French economist Jacques Attali.[52]

This proliferation modifies geo-social and geo-economic landscapes for the future. It makes us rethink the notion of traditional borders, countries, and trade regulations in order to adjust to these new fluid groups.

The creative community is a family:

Sharing is an important pillar for a truly creative group. Artists gravitate toward and stimulate each other.

We create a cloud-tribe of polyvalent individuals, an orb of people with different sets of skills and common global values. As in a family, we can argue and clash, as long as we maintain a connection based on love, respect for each other's unique expression, and exchange of creative resources.

Inclusive rather than exclusive:

Like-minded individuals flock toward each other around common poles of interests. Private societies and congregations sprout throughout history. Clubs fulfill one's desire to be part of a group. Some of these guilds have demonstrated their ability to promote the creativity of the group as well as that of each person's successfully, especially when creativity was posed as a priority. The legendary rap band the Wu-Tang Clan assembled in 1993 on New York City's Staten Island as a loose congregation of nine MCs to establish a collective force and spin off as many side projects as possible through each individual member. This visionary initiative started a movement that allowed many young rap artists to voice their opinions and improve their personal and social living conditions since then.

A community achieves a greater social standard when it caters to individual *and* collective interests at the same time. The *exclusive* modus operandi—one *or* the other—is abandoned to the benefit of the *inclusive* modus operandi—one *and* the other. The society of the future no longer needs to divide to better reign.

Putting creativity before greed:

Deeply anchored in our psyche is the belief that there is not enough for everybody. The neighbor is a threat, therefore we must amass to prevent famine, malady, and extinction; we must conquer and kill for the sake of the lineage.

The potlatch model, the primary economic system adopted by pre-Columbian indigenous tribes in the Pacific Northwest, is a gift-giving ceremony where a clan or chieftan, seeking influence, gives away valuable goods. (It was also known to sometimes deliberately destroy valuables as a show of wealth, an extreme particularly disturbing for those in need, so we will rather focus here on the give-away aspect). A shared economy reuses excess products and services and redistributes excess gains instead of hoarding them. Where idle assets serve only a few, the re-injection of valuables into the circle of design, production, distribution, trade, and consumption insures economic and social momentum, fairness, and minimal waste. Fringe benefits of a share-based system include full participation and a general feeling of safety with which the collectivity becomes supportive, and complies to pay tax contributions in good spirit since it approves and seals what tax money is used for.

The time has come to invert our priorities and put creativity before fear, and collaboration before competition.

From worth to wealth:

We are reconsidering the measurement tools of our economic performance. Abundance can be redefined in many ways beyond material goods and services. There is money, there is time, there is labor, and there is creativity, which is tantamount to worth and by extension, wealth.

Fearless of copy:

As long as our creative drive is thriving, new wealth is generated, and there is plenty for everyone; scarcity loosens its grip, the fear of lacking has nothing left to feed on, and greed withers and dies.

We create endlessly. This aptitude constitutes an antidote to the issue of copy and counterfeit. Those who spend a lifetime birthing brilliant ideas should see their proprietary rights protected and be allowed to take well-deserved rests throughout their career; multiple births take a toll on the mother's body. Yet a creator can only spend so much time fighting the copycats: the more vehement our resistance, the more painful the experience, and the less time we have to create. It is less of a pain to instead keep our creation rate high enough so that it out-runs counterfeiters. The most efficient and natural form of immunity is to boost our creativity drive.

Service, generosity, and security:

The eighty-first and last text of the *Tao Te Ching* links the concept of knowledge with that of service, generosity and security. I am particularly interested in the last four verses that conclude this epic and sage collection of poems; they warn of hoarding and foster the redistribution of excess profit:

> True words are not fancy.
>
> Fancy words are not true.
>
> The good do not debate.

Debaters are not good.

The one who really knows is not broadly learned,

The extensively learned do not really know.

The sage does not hoard,

She gives people her surplus.

Giving her surplus to others she is enriched.

The way of Heaven is to help and not harm.[53]

The modern ruler's virtues:

Leadership is redefined today with a new generation of CEOs considering values and ethics over power and profit at all costs.

The traits characterizing leadership have been amply studied. In his theory of the theatrics of leaderships, David M. Boje, Professor of Management at New Mexico State University, synthetizes the four profiles that modern leaders perform under, based on the precepts of Italian statesman Niccolò Machiavelli, German philosopher Friedrich Nietzsche, German sociologist Max Weber, and American political historian James McGregor Burns. The archetypal profiles are the Prince, the "Übermensch" or Superman/Superwoman, the Bureaucrat or Transactional Leader, and the Hero or Transformational Leader,[54] operating respectively through the virtues of charisma, fortitude, vision, and service. Rulers throughout history operate through a combination of these various archetypes. Today, however, the crowd demands the highest expression of management to be vested in service. Empathetic leaders in touch with the welfare of their followers perform better and stay in place longer in an age where democratization follows naturally the flow of information transparency.

Servitude is a choice; like a Cancer-type zodiacal personality, a humane boss listens and makes decisions for the group that transcend his or her personal interests or those of only a few.[55]

Organic leadership:

Our project helps those interested in leading to cross-check their values and apply them in their enterprises. When a user creates a group (orb) on our digital platform, he or she invites participants to join, and is by default designated as the ruler of the group. If the ruler fails to honor the best interests of the group, members simply leave. The system allows for a natural selection of decision-makers.

Leading by example:

"Do as I do" is a popular phrase in the business press these days. By opposition, the authoritarian recommendation "do as I say" now lacks convincing power. Leaders build credibility and a following when they act as role models based on their actions. Since our purpose is to discuss fundamentals, I will take here three classical examples.

The principle of *Satyagraha,* from Sanskrit *satya* for *truth* and *āgraha* for *obstinacy*, was made popular by Mahatma Gandhi when he marched in civil resistance for India's independence. In Gandhi's words, Satyagraha stems from love: "Truth (satya) implies love, and firmness (āgraha) engenders and therefore serves as a synonym for force. I thus began to call the Indian movement Satyagraha, that is to say, the Force which is born of Truth and Love or non-violence, and gave up the use of the phrase "passive resistance [...]."[56]

Nelson Mandela led his peaceful action to end apartheid in South Africa with a forgiving heart: "It was during those long and lonely years that my hunger for the freedom of my own people became a hunger for the freedom of all people, black and white. I knew as well as I knew anything that the oppressor must be liberated just as surely as the oppressed. A man who takes away another man's freedom is a prisoner of hatred, he is locked behind the bars of prejudice an narrow-mindedness."[57]

As Martin Luther King, Jr. stated: "People are often led to causes and often become committed to great ideas through persons who personify those ideas. They have to find the embodiment of the idea in flesh and blood in order to commit themselves to it."[58]

Those leaders worked with high stakes. Yet there is no leadership too small to be considered. Dr. King famously said of humble progress:

"If you can't fly then run, if you can't run then walk, if you can't walk then crawl, but whatever you do you have to keep moving forward."[59]

These examples of leadership are made possible by the forces of truth, love, and determination. Credibility is built in the unwavering belief in one's values. But more interestingly, beyond the sacrifice stand creative and emotional qualities.

Redefining the masculine ideal:

Poetry, beauty, and humanity are values for a male leader, too.

In addition to their talent for leadership, Mr. Mandela and Dr. King were great poets: They used metaphors to convey their thoughts, which made their profound statements even more beautiful. Their creative expression made their leadership memorable and popular as they showed their human face in adversity. These role models have demonstrated that vulnerability and an artistic ability are virtues for a man as well. It is noteworthy that these two go hand-in-hand.

Softer and emotional values are traditionally attributed to women and children. In many societies we still think that virility is tough and unbending; it is stuck in a rigid image of performance and over-achievement. We live in a patriarchal society where the masculine has been restricted and perverted to debilitation. It deviated into a symbol for power and domination, blocking the flow of creativity. Feminism is a counterbalance to machismo. It exists sometimes in radical forms, and necessarily so; women's right to vote in the northern hemisphere is barely a century old. We will discuss the concept of the feminine further in chapter 8.

The original intention of the patriarchy was to provide security for the tribe; it wasn't meant to write off understanding and empathy. Men and women must work together to correct the course and enhance female values through their leaderships.

Honoring one's word is regal:

The sharing economy[60] is also called the peer-to-peer economy, where each participant has the possibility to communicate face to face. Honesty has more chances when people talk directly to each other. We wouldn't need so many layers of regulation if we had the ability to honor our word and seal more deals on a handshake. On the

Magna Carta of globalization, we grow estranged from each other; we lose our touch, twist our tongue and compromise ourselves. Direct communication gives us our word back.

Lack of consensus leads to sabotage:

Managers know that a company will fail when the ruler recurrently makes decisions against the recommendation of its board of executives. Coworkers will resent their bosses' poor decisions and energetically act against the interest of the company, even without intention to do so. It is a human trait to want to be right; the "I told you so" syndrome ultimately equates to sabotage.

A round table offers each participant a direct link:

In a pyramidal structure, visibility is obstructed between the base and the top. Layers of hierarchical categories block the flow of information. A circular structure offers the members of a community an open view from all vantage points. Our wheel configuration is a round table that eliminates the risk of poor translations between each of its twelve values or between members.

The wheel repartition also enables the moderating process of an internal debate. Users are the queens of their own wheel and kings to their personal projects. They sit in the center with the task to lead the creative voices within one's personality. They make sure that each value gets a chance to be expressed, and know how to crack a friendly whip when one of them attempts a coup to take over the crown. The center of the wheel is the pacifying meeting point of our inner democracy.

The circular use of resources:

The theory of circular economy[61] invites us to observe the planet's living systems and apply its cyclical mechanisms to our own industrial economy. The linear conventional industrial processes that consists of extracting resources, producing things, and throwing them away not only depletes finite resources but creates excess garbage. Re-using in one way or another is the solution. Outgrowths of circular economy include propositions such as Cradle To Cradle (1976),[62] Biomimicry, and Industrial Ecology.

We find efficient and resilient solutions to the depletion of natural resources by observing diversity in nature. The concept of the Blue Economy[63] stresses how abundant the planet is in offering natural solutions; not only can we make do with what we have, but we can also create new wealth in building upon what already exists. We can adapt these principles to our creativity and get inspired to upcycle unused ideas or let the community do it, provided we are willing to give away our surplus and let another dispose of what we do not need at the moment.

Cross-pollination of creativity, an under-used goldmine:

Creativity feeds creativity. Once we feel safe to share ideas, an interesting phenomenon happens: Our peers can reflect our concepts back to us in their own language. Most of us have learned a work language based on the category of business we trained in, with a technical jargon and specific wording that can hold a totally different definition once extracted from its original professional context. The word *cloud* evokes a different meaning for poets, meteorologists, or digital developers. There is a tremendous potential in this diversity that is not commonly used in today's corporate discussions. Indeed, the various interpretations can be bounced from one profession to the other in a way that catalyzes a new perspective. The technician can carve a manual of instructions inspired by the cook's recipes. The financier will tailor an income plan out of harvest patterns in nature. The martial artist can choreograph his fight routine based on the ballet dancer's aesthetics. A computer chip circuitry can be inspired by the way a healer channels universal energy, and so forth. We will explore the mechanisms of this analogical process further in chapter 5.

The field of possibilities offered for projects created by multi-facetted individuals is amplified. Fertilization takes place in the Holy Grail represented by our wheel of values.

This project presents an abstract ensemble of circles and concentric wheels, each with their cogs and turns that can connect to stimulate hybrid creative propositions in the user's mind. The loop of the circle configuration symbolizes the possibility for recycling budding ideas into their best expression by bouncing them from one value to the other, or from one user to the other.

It is the wheel we use to gather in our Hall of FAMILY.

This is a COMMUNITY.

The fourth set of values calls for an online application to create groups, or orbs.

It describes our level of ownership of a project (owner, member), and our level of privacy (private, groups only, public).

Managerial, amenable and sharing, the psychological archetype matching this part of our personality is THE QUEEN/KING.

5

WILL

EXPANDING OUR CREATIVE VISION

ART, CREATIVITY, JOY, ABUNDANCE, UTOPIA

We relinquished our creativity in order to belong:

Belongingness is a basic emotional need. We need to feel a part of the group. In every society, starting with ostracism in Ancient Greece, banishment was a severe punishment; in medieval Europe those banned lost their assets and rights to legal protection, becoming prey to crime, and had little chance of being accepted by another community.[64] In order to belong, we have compromised ourselves. We taught ourselves to stay in line and because of this we have learned to dislike difference.

We have bullied oddness so that it folds back into the mold. We have ostracized the eccentric until it denied its wild nature. We sold our soul to obedience and rewarded ourselves with gold and affection when we fitted to the norm; out of disbelief, we betrayed our truth and forced the neighbor to abdicate in turn. We deprived ourselves of the ability to fashion our own narratives. Story-less and faceless, we have lived another's story. The governing powers we set in place, with the help of the media we keep alive, fed us their tales and we made them our own. We turned sad in sameness. Normality became a tragedy.

Reclaiming our emotions:

Revolts took place many times through philosophy and art.

As a reaction to the dehumanization triggered by the Industrial Revolution (c. 1712–c.1840) and in the face of the threat of uniformity in a machine-driven society, the European intelligentsia of the

Romantic period sparked a humanist movement to reinstate emotions as a force to generate beauty in art and speech.

At the beginning of the twentieth century, the Russian mystic Gurdjieff was teaching self-observation, "work on oneself,"[65] to his followers as a method to wake up from universal somnambulism and to societal laws that are detrimental to self-expression.

Little by little, we started to explore our complexities and admit that emotions are no longer a menace to the functioning of society.

Embracing fear:

To be prepared for the worst, we work and make money; we are over-insured and backed by our lawmen in all sectors of our lives.

Our minds keep a tight grip on our present while devising strategies for our future. Our financial and economic systems bear witness to our need for control; our stock market has turned into an intricate maze of speculation. In attempting to predict the value of future commodities, the game ends up influencing and ruling tomorrow's gains, artificially inflating its importance in our daily lives. We try to manipulate every detail in our surroundings. We expect disaster and we jam-pack our schedules, leaving no space for novelty. Our children are over-booked with activities and therefore inhibited in their creative skills. We don't trust them to wander around and make their own discoveries because we don't trust the environment or neighbors who could be psychotic criminals.

But we are becoming aware of the paralyzing upshots of our fear of a doomed world. After all, it is tragicomical that what we want from money is to have enough to never have to think about it, and what we want from insurance policies is to never have to use them.

The nature of abundance:

As mentioned in chapter 1, we are beings in the process of expansion. We are designed in and for abundance, and the universe in turn is highly responsive; it mirrors back our ability to be generous. What we focus on resonates at a certain frequency and attracts a similar vibration. There is a conspiracy to honor our deepest and sometimes unformulated inclinations. Our wishes are granted. We are masterful creators, and one of our mighty fears is to transgress our own power.

We create what we feed:

We create so well that we equally have the power to create an abundance of great things as we have the power to create an abundance of lack—lack of love, lack of money, lack of time, lack of health, and so forth. Focusing on war makes the news, heats up the discussion, and reinforces the concept. Intrigue feeds more intrigue. If one speaks illness, illness echoes, more people hear it, and it grows conviction power. Un-creations are creations, too. What the universe responds to is the content and the intensity of our concentrated attention, not the *not* part. The universe doesn't hear negation. It works in absolute value.

Opening up to receiving:

Giving is a relief for the highly creative beings that we are. A nursing mother bursting with milk must feed her child. We must give lest we become overtaken with our own fullness. Prolific as we are, we are thankful to find a receptacle in which to spill our creative bounty. Unexpressed creativity is a burden at best and gangrene at worst.

Generosity is a two-way street, and sometimes it is harder to receive than to give: It means opening our door to take in another's creation. It might feel like an intrusion. Biological, mental, or emotional, penetration can make us receptive or reluctant, depending on life experience and culture; becoming the outlet for someone's intent exposes us. It takes self-work to be courageous, discerning, and to grant oneself the authorization to welcome abundance. It takes nerves to say yes.

Cosmic R.O.I:

We reap what we sow, and we forget to connect the happy dots. We are learning to grow our understanding of how cause and effect interact. The spectrum of return can be so large that we don't always establish a link between what we send out and what we get back. If I decide one day to not charge a particular client for my educational services, while checking my emails to find that I won a complimentary one-to-one class at the computer store, my mind won't necessarily establish the connection between both occurrences. The computer store email was sent before I decided to work for free, therefore it couldn't have been a favor returned. Yet I can choose to bypass the logic of linear time and decide that it is my recompense. This is just one example of the endless ways that the universe can reward us, and we couldn't imagine all the miraculous possibilities even if we tried. The sky is the limit. Our power of creating is only limited by our imagination. It is uplifting beyond words to look at our actions with this particular lens on cosmic return on investment. We become the instigators of our own rewarding system.

It is our duty to share our gifts:

We must believe that our inner light exists, and that it is ours legitimately. Accepting our brightness is a challenge. We are luminous beings and we don't dare to believe in our divinity. We have no reasons to feel repressed and frightful. More and more, people are awakening to their creative gift and eccentricity is no longer witch-hunted. We have no reason to be shy. There is no arrogance in stepping up, quite the opposite; it is a waste to not deliver ourselves. The world awaits our contribution toward global ascension and the betterment of society. Everyone holds a piece of heaven on earth and of the future of humanity, no matter how large or shiny the piece.

Bold to shine:

It takes courage to step up in the limelight and speak our own name. Offering our creativity and innermost treasures to the whole wide world is an act of bravura. We feel vulnerable to potential judgment. Criticism starts within; we can be our worst enemy when we allow our mind arbiter to pull up the red card and send our rising gifts to the bench for the rest of the game. The road to creative fulfillment has a few bumps.

Fear of failure:

Fear of failure is a big impediment to creativity. We are afraid to be ridiculed, rejected, fired. We worry that our creations are not new. We are scared of being outdone by someone else.

We don't want to be smothered and discouraged from creating again. It takes faith to overcome failure; when we open-source our creativity, we give away an intimate part of ourselves. The fragile flame needs shielding from the big bad jealous wolf and the abrasive blows of criticism.

A creative failure is already forgiven:

Battle wounds come with exploring and manifesting; we get big scars when we out-brave ourselves, when we bite off more than we can chew, and small bruises when we tiptoe into the shallow waters of our desires. There are no losers, only heroic go-getters or cautious experimentalists.

In the creative process we can test ourselves, trip and redress, recur or move on. Many successful businesspeople will tell you proudly how they went through bankruptcy, sometimes repeatedly, and got back on their feet; they respect the experience and are in turn respected for it. I find America to be a place that is understanding of failure, where people can be less intimidated about taking creative risks.

The power in utopia:

Many great visionaries who have impacted the world by their discoveries started with a utopian ideology. A very young John Keats honors classic Greek Idealism in his poem *Ode on a Grecian Urn*:

> When old age shall this generation waste,
>
> Thou shalt remain, in midst of other woe
>
> Than ours, a friend to man, to whom thou say'st,
>
> "Beauty is truth, truth beauty,—that is all
>
> Ye know on earth, and all ye need to know."[66]

Cynics will argue that idealism and beauty feel safe in the naivety of the youth. Utopia has many critics, starting with Sir Thomas More, the English lawyer, statesman, and humanist philosopher who coined the term for his own fictional political essay of the same name. In *The Utopia* (1516), More depicts an ideological society with goals unattainable in the religious, political, and ethical context in which it was written.

Nevertheless, what we feed, we make real; when we stand for the hope of improvement, soon enough the hundredth monkey tips over the scales of manifestation in favor of our ideal. We can choose to be the visionaries of unformed beauty. Belief in a utopia sets the tone for transformation, doubt tests it, consensus validates it.

Doubt is an agent for creativity:

When we form fear in our mind, when we doubt a desired outcome, we send our hopes away from our earthly potential to another reality. All the thoughts and intents we have had are not wasted; they move to probabilities where we exist concurrently, where we enjoy perfect health, a perfect body, and perfect relationships, where we can always access them and make them our own. But we test them. The line is thin between cynicism, the great abortionist, and constructive criticism, the common feature of our mind and the lantern for discernment. Our intellect wants to serve us and make conscious choices for survival and enjoyment.

Doubt is the stumbling block that forces us to stand our ground. It designs ropes for the ring of our debates. It provokes us to invent solutions. Resistance triggers creativity and builds up stamina.

Create first, money and time will follow:

Two concerns are particularly crippling in the beginning of the creative process: money and time. A lack of funds and of duration to implement our ideas impairs the creative process if we make it our priority. If we first let creation express itself, putting the "what" before the "how," we give it all its chances to grow strong. If we focus next on the manner in which our creation benefits others, we give it even more strength. Self-fulfillment and service become our priorities.

Only then can the practical details of implementation be addressed. Money and time, often joined at the hip, are the sponsors of our creations more than they are their components. Surely they will smell the bacon and make a grand entrance into the life of a project once the idea is solid. When the product is gold, help is on the way. "Leap, and the net will appear," recommends writer Julia Cameron in *The Artist's Way, a Spiritual Path to Higher Creativity,* a twelve-step manual to creative recovery that has inspired millions of people worldwide since 1992.

The power of imagination and hypothesis:

Sir James George Frazer, one of the fathers of modern anthropology, claimed in praise of science "that human belief progresses through three stages: primitive magic, replaced by religion, in turn replaced by science."[67]

Precisely: Science is predominant today in our system of thinking, to the point of being revered and even idolized. Empiricism prematurely dismisses our dreams. When we discard what is not demonstrated, we narrow our potential, we obliterate intuition, and we waste an occasion to stimulate our imagination. Renowned scientists are great poets when they speculate.

Starting a team discussion with *"imagine that . . ."*, or *"take for granted that . . ."*, brings stunning results. Those words have the power to defuse reasonability and bypass conventions. Hypothesis works like a charm. We can be apprentice sorcerers uninhibited by the word *if* should we choose to be.

I must say that this statement is a disclaimer for this book, which wouldn't exist without postulates.

Analogy as a method:

When I was a child in France, we would play a game called *Si j'étais . . . , or* If I was . . . . Equivalent to the English version Who Am I, it is a charade game where one person mentally chooses a famous character. The others guess the character's identity using analogies. The guess is encouraged by describing what color, what animal, what place, what type of food, what time period and so on this character would correspond to, until the proper answer is found.

Our wheel of values acts like a game of *Si j'étais*; it facilitates the formation of metaphors in the user's perception. It encourages the mind to cross-fertilize ideas. Analogy can be taught to stimulate one's creativity, using pictures, sounds, and words as memory triggers.

No goal, no expectation:

Our project uses the energy of the number 5, odd number of freedom and exhilaration, affiliated with the myth of the constellation of the lion and the zodiac sign of Leo. Leo beams like its ruling star the Sun. It warms up everything that comes near. Its magnifying force is unstoppable. It loves to create and procreate. Joy is glamorous and gets things done! Every ideation session I have participated in so far using this value system has been great fun for the participants, and has brought amazing results.

Creation bypasses the mind's expectations. The mind wants things for us. It plans the outcome of our creative effort. Is it trying to help creation? The potential is so vast. The mind is not qualified to see it all, so it must surrender to a more powerful entity. Spirit takes over to guide us. The one who starts coaching ends up writing. The book becomes a film. The film is the centerpiece of an event. The event turns into a product . . . .

Commitment to our art:

Genius is fierce. But talent is not enough: it demands a workout every now and then. We flourish when we devote ourselves wholly to our creativity. Exercise unpacks genius. Industriousness polishes brilliance. The hobby turns into an art. Art becomes a job. We are professional artists clocking in each day at the factory of our own making.

Regularly recording our creative progression in a journal will help us to fine-tune our art and give it the central throne in our lives. Plus, it's fun.

Reflecting the grace within:

Being creative is being oneself 100 percent. Creations come to manifestation when they fully match the vibration of their creator: being oneself *is* the ultimate creation.

Grace is achieved with the exact reflection of pure truth, no matter how pretty the mind judges the image to be. Completion occurs when the creation wholly matches the identity of its creator. Taste, a subjective elitist, doesn't have a say here.

Creativity transcends time:

When we're bored, we keep looking at the clock and minutes seem like hours. We feel as though we're aging faster and the perception of time is dense, heavy. But when engaged in creative activities, time snaps by as if it never existed. When we love what we do, we lose ourselves. We step out of time, an indicator that we are in touch with the creative spark within. We look refreshed, we feel energetic and available to others; when we go to bed at night, we feel the satisfaction of a day well spent.

When we bend time, we build our own pace, we design our calendar. The surrender to our creativity feels like a fountain of youth. Joy is a constant in the realm where time doesn't exist.

The path of passion:

Joy-driven activities are undervalued because they can seem unrelated to what we think we should be doing. We can be harsh in denying excitement to ourselves when it seems unproductive. We write joy off as kid's play and tell ourselves to grow up. We miss all the fun, and we pass an opportunity to create something that can one day turn into a full-time job or even a lucrative business. We separate leisure and work, where they could be one and the same. Business is everybody's business; our work life can become one of passion.

When we learn to trust the timing and "follow our bliss," as states mythologist Joseph Campbell,[68] we discover that we have a genuine instinct for what makes us happy. Excitement overthrows reason and joy supplants dullness.

Are we ready for joy?

We are afraid to let our joy run wild. Joy is a driving force. Society has dismissed ecstasy as madness. Etymologically, ecstasy is derived from Greek *ekstasis,* meaning *standing out of the self,* as if fulfillment could only be attained by stepping out of our functional human shell. By associating extreme pleasure with some form of trance, we make it spooky and inaccessible. We talk ourselves out of the voodoo.

Psychoanalyst and sexuality expert Wilhelm Reich received the cold shoulder in the European and American medical community in the 1930–40s when he publicized the concept of *orgone*, a word contracted from *orgasm* and *organism*, to describe a form of euphoric ethereal energy that has healing power. Controversial then, Reich stretched minds; he would probably have been welcomed with open arms during the sexual revolution of the 1970s. He was sentenced to jail in 1956, where he died. To some martial arts practitioners, this ethereal energy simply refers to *qi*, or *chi*, a much more benign terminological choice. God forbid we have fun. Happy people are hard to manipulate indeed.

But we are also afraid to like happiness so much that it becomes an addiction. In a compulsion to keep society in check, we have repressed the display of our sexuality and our creativity. It is no surprise that we feel the urge to reclaim bliss as our own, and seek the experience of it. To this effect, a solid training in indulgence can help us demystify the fright we have to lose ourselves in pleasure.

It takes courage to unleash our impulses and experiment with extreme joy.

Creating as a solemn ritual:

Religious or not, rituals are solemn ceremonies.

In chapter 3, we mentioned *theurgy* as being one on the three pillars of Hermeticism. When we create our own ceremony to request a particular outcome to a situation, we infuse it with intent. Sacred, it becomes a personal prayer; the more solemn the energy we launch in the atmosphere, the more powerful it becomes. A ritual becomes a creation in itself when it is custom-tailored to the unique need of an individual.

We can introduce ritualistic practices for our art in our daily work routine. Art becomes a means by which we connect our spirit to our physical reality.

The power of prayer:

It is said that holding a prayer in our thoughts for seven seconds gives it power to come to life. Maintaining focus on our dreams for an extended period of time invokes matching energies, and is therefore instrumental to their manifestation. When we rest in prayer the universe takes charge; facts and things fall into place beyond our active involvement. Our trust plants certainty and miracles occur.

Creativity is our livelihood:

We are amorphous clay in the hands of creation. It seeks us as much as we seek it. We possess free will, and we want to trust that our malleability will be used in the service of our happiness.

Abundance is waiting for us in the form of pleasant working conditions, glowing health, fulfilling relationships, and material beauties. We creators deserve to make a pleasant and successful living out of our creativity.

Empowering team members to turn their brand around:

In the context of a brand restructuring, stellar results are obtained when employees are behind the steering wheel and work as a team. Who knows a brand and its products better than its own members? The system of values works as a companion; it can be calibrated to become an in-house creative facilitator, while providing the expert eye of an outsider.

This tool can be used for team cohesion as well, when the morale of a team is low.

An ideation session to create a product, a case study:

I used the system of values as a moderating tool for an ideation session with a New York-based manufacturer of beauty products. The creative discussion started with a philosophical approach to define the twelve values relevant for the development of a new cosmetic formula.

As the conversation evolved, the definition was calibrated with concrete words matching the brand's specific corporate language, products, and manufacturing processes, based on the input of everyone involved. The team of eight members included product development, marketing, and research and development, including several chemists.

Each party was reunited around a common goal and was involved all the way from the inception of the project until the completion of the task. The solid foundation of a product was collectively established in one day, to the satisfaction of all. Team members all felt enthusiasm and a sense of purpose.

This project offers a recreational environment to the kids at heart that we are. Colorful, endlessly surprising, this playground encourages self-expression. We find ourselves in the process to be much more creative and free than we thought we were. Work turns into an exciting game in constant regeneration: we lose ourselves in the game of work.

It is the display we need in our Hall of ARTS & ENTERTAINMENT.

This is a PLAY.

The fifth set of values calls for a tool to allow the association of ideas through word combinations. It is a cross-pollination application that allows analogy and hybrid concepts to be formed. It is a methodology for metaphors.

Prolific, generous, and larger than life, the psychological archetype matching this part of our personality is THE LOVER.

6

ANALYZE

STRUCTURING OUR CREATIVE VISION

ORGANIZATION, NUMBERS, DETAILS, PURPOSE, SERVICE

Numbers are an omnipresent abstraction:

Numbers represent the nomenclature chosen to establish the foundation for this project.

From one to two to infinity and back, numbers quantify; that's their job. They give their components to the formulas of life.

Mathematically, creatures are creations derived from numbers in a rhythm. Like geometry, numbers infuse everything, rain or shine: the mass of things, the definition of space, the flow of molecules rushing through our veins, the choice of words, the whisper of a voice, the fear of losing a loved one, the warmth of someone's glow, the weight of heritage, the quantification of change, the fate of stock market analysis.

Numero-logic:

Numbers hold power, culturally if nothing else. They have been distilled and monetized at length from calculus to biology, from probability to metaphysics, by thinkers laying out the connection between waveform and particle, between abstraction and matter.

Numerology finds its source with Pythagoras, who believed that all things and events inherent to human life had numerical relationships.

Numbers give their name to the fourth book of the Hebrew Bible; the Babylonians, the early Greeks, the Hindu scriptures and the Tao have also crowned them as rulers of fate. Modern mathematics refers to numerology as a pseudoscience. Numbers are concepts and it is interesting to consider the logic contained within their energy.

At this point in our reflection, this project has momentum with the number 1, resources with the number 2, magic with the number 3, a loving container with the number 4, and artfulness with the number 5. Now it needs a structure with the number 6.

The number 6 in number theory, being equal to the sum of its proper positive divisors 1, 2, and 3, is the smallest perfect[69] number. We want to look at the strategic aspect of this perfection to serve our structure for creative personal and business applications.

Astrology is a technique:

Western astrology is amply referenced in this material, and I would like to take some time to discuss its structure. The etymological schism between *astronomy*, describing the movement of the stars, and its cousin *astrology*, describing their influence, officially began in the late 1400s. The scientific revolution and the intellectual movement of the Enlightenment confirmed the difference in the mid-seventeenth century in Europe. From ancient times until the scholastic period the border between the two notions wasn't clear. While the twelve zodiac sign language originates from ancient Babylonia, as described in detail in Jack Lindsay's *Origins of Astrology*, ancient Greek philosophers considered cosmology to be in relation to human consciousness. Nicholas Campion, historian of astrology and cultural astronomy, notes that: "Even though Plato had little to say about astrology, his other statements about the stars were to become the foundation of Western tradition."[70]

Astronomer Claudius Ptolemaeus is thought to have written, in the second century B.C., a treatise on mathematics and ancient Greek astronomy, *The Almagestum*, based on Aristotle's cosmology and an early foundation for the geocentric twelve-house Western astrology structured as we know it today. The twelve signs are ruled by planets in the solar system. The Assyrians observing the heavens saw formations resembling animals like a bull, a lion, and a scorpion, yet we owe our modern astrological characteristics to the Greeks and the Romans, who gave zodiacal constellations their mythical traits. In folk culture multiple interpretations have been derived on the characteristics attached to the twelve symbols, which can be animals (for instance, crab for Cancer), human impersonations (maiden for Virgo), chimeras (Centaur for Sagittarius), or objects (scales for Libra), which have seduced the popular psyche to the point of superstition when claiming their divinatory powers.

Dismissing astrology:

As early as the mid-third century B.C., writings about star-gazing and associated human moods are common in Rome. Critics of these folk beliefs abound: the Roman statesman Cicero quotes the poet Ennius who repeats frequently Achilles' words in Euripides' *Iphigenia:*[71] "They note the astrologic signs of heaven whenever the Goats or Scorpions of great Jove or other monstrous names of brutish forms rise in the Zodiac. But no one regards the sensible facts of earth on which we tread while gazing on the starry prodigies."

Astrologers were expulsed from Rome in 150 B.C.; an ordinance was issued against astrologers and sorcerers by the emperor Agrippa in 33 B.C. Prophetic and divining books were burned by emperor Octavian.[72]

Throwing out the baby with the bathwater:

Even if astrology is trivialized throughout history by folk belief and deformed all too often into superstition, its roots in the observation of the gravitational and nuclear influences of celestial bodies on earth and by extension on human beings deserve to be considered. Robert O. Becker, M.D., a researcher in cell regeneration, notes in his book *The Body Electric: Electromagnetism and the Foundation of Life:* "The earth's magnetic field is largely a result of interaction between the magnetic field per se, emanating from the planet's molten iron-nickel core, and the charged gas of the ionosphere. It varies with the lunar day and month, and there's also a yearly change as we revolve around the sun."[73]

In the 1920s, social reformer anthroposophist Rudolph Steiner developed biodynamic agriculture, a method of organic farming using an astrological sowing and planting calendar based on the observation of lunar phases and planetary cycles. Even if performance in comparison to other forms of organic agriculture is still inconclusive today, biodynamic agriculture is used in 47 countries, with Germany accounting for 45.1 percent of the world's biodynamic hectares.[74] Well, if Germany likes it . . . .

On the subject of astrology, Jack Lindsay concludes:

Again we are faced by the paradox that at the heart of the irrational elements in astrology there lay what was the most valuable aspect of ancient thought—the sense of being organically part of a living universe. A key-problem for the modern world is to regain what was valid and creative in this sense without yielding to the irrational elements.[75]

Guided by myth:

The philosopher and theologian St. Thomas Aquinas, who synthetized Aristotelian concepts and shaped modern philosophy, acknowledged the influence of astrology when he suggested that "Divination by the stars is not unlawful," while cautioning about its predictive aspects.[76] So does psychologist C. G. Jung, who used cosmology and mythology in the shaping of his psychological archetypes. Jung concluded that:

Astrology would be an example of synchronicity on a grand scale if only there were enough thoroughly tested findings to support it. But at least we have at our disposal a number of well-tested and statistically verifiable facts which make the problem of astrology seem worthy of scientific investigation. Its value is obvious to the psychologist, since astrology represents the sum of all the psychological knowledge of Antiquity.[77]

For the sake of scientific evidence we dismiss too easily the human desire to belong, as well as the creative potential hidden in folk culture and imagination as evoked by myths. Myths make history as well as facts, as we will discuss in chapter 9 referring to the works of philosopher Michel Foucault. As French semiotician Roland Barthes stated, a myth is a "type of speech, a system of communication, a message," and as such can take any form: oral, written, and photography, cinema, reporting, sport, shows, or publicity.[78]

Our project uses values based on mythical characteristics.

An analytical approach:

The sixth sign of the zodiac follows the myth of the constellation of Virgo the virgin, and is believed in Western astrology to be ruled by the planet Mercury. Its symbol is pictured on the Tree of Life as the Twentieth Path, the Path of Intelligence of Will.[79]

There is a close correspondence between the Tree of Life and the mystical Tarot's major Arcana. In the Tarot, the Twentieth Path corresponds to major Arcanum The Hermit and expresses one's dedication to introspection. The Hermit is the torchbearer showing the way to spirituality, while staying connected to the material world:

> Think of me as a teacher, counselor, therapist, or spirit guide [...] Using my principles of patience, contemplation, and examination before action, you can step back from troubling situations and see them from a broader perspective. [...] [c]onsider the real purpose of your daily activities and set high standards for business operations. Does your work contribute to general welfare? Does it add meaning to your life? Will the part you play provide a model for others to follow?
>
> My key phrase is light of the higher ways.[80]

The energy of the Virgo expresses humility and stands for service. It cleans up and heals its environment. Its ruler Mercury is associated with the intellect. Virgo pays great attention to details and seeks purity and perfection. It is concerned with strategy and structure.

Numbers provide a structure.

Numbers as a strategy:

The zodiac circle is composed of two sets of six distinct entities, expressing the duality of the material world. The six first signs are more of an introversive nature, and they face the six other signs that are more of an extroversive nature. For instance, the first sign of the zodiac is Aries, number 1 for identity and interaction with the self, and stands diametrically opposed to the sign of Libra, number 7 symbolizing partnership and interaction with another.

On the astrological wheel, the sixth sign of earthy Virgo crystallizes analytical qualities, and stands across the sign of Pisces and its watery diffusive nature.

The rule of twelve reconciles two blocks of six echoing each other in symmetrical complementarity.

Twelve is just right:

We will explore the number 12 deeper in the twelfth chapter; but since 12 is 6 x 2, let me make a few remarks on the subject in this chapter on structure. Many twelve-step programs help people quit addictions or improve performance; they produce mixed results and their efficacy has not been proven. Nevertheless, the choice of twelve, in number and in concept, provides a balanced quantity of options to categorize our values: plenty of room to create and enough boundaries to not get lost. Just right between rejecting and overdoing; just right between physical reality and higher consciousness.

I am exploring how we can apply the symbolism contained in these numbers as a filing system for our values.

A foundation based on archetypes:

I suggest that these values, associated with numbers, also pair with archetypal characters: from one to twelve we find respectively the Warrior, the Artisan, the Messenger, the Ruler, the Lover, the Server, the Juggler, the Transformer, the Scholar, the Merchant, the Traveler and the Healer.

An archetype is a primordial model used as a source reference.

C. G. Jung used archetypal human portraits based on mythology and alchemy to describe various psychological traits in the collective unconscious:[81] "The Collective unconscious is a part of the psyche which can be negatively distinguished from a personal unconscious by the fact that it does not, like the latter, owe its existence to personal experience and consequently is not a personal acquisition. [...] Whereas the personal unconscious consists for the most part of *complexes*, the content of the collective unconscious is made up essentially of *archetypes*."

Philosophers and psychologists find archetypes value-able, reconciling the domains of thoughts with those of feelings and spiritualism.

The notion of archetype is generic and global; therefore it leaves room for impersonation and imagination.

In our project, we can use the list of archetypes as a means for identification, classification of creative itches, and integration of the various parts of the persona. *Complex* turns into *complete*, and beautifully so.

A frame to organize our hobbies and passions:

The astrological house systems organize twelve categories affecting human life in a wheel structure. Let's put our values on a similar wheel.

I choose to develop a fuller life, I make this affirmation my goal, and I place it in the center of my wheel. In doing so, I create my desired reality. I call in all my joy, my passions and skills, my long-forgotten dreams, my abandoned wishes, to craft a unique living experience that is exciting to me.

A guideline proves to be useful in order to visualize the many layers of our longings, with their accents, twists, and complexities.

Dreaming our own wheel of fortune:

Users are engaged to define their aspirations on that wheel, as if they were asking themselves what they would do if they won the lottery. Answering such a question is the most uplifting process. It sends any blockage to the doghouse, and helps us to get out of our own way, while we drift into a delightful reverie of our ideal life. We are the inspired gardeners on our personal wheel.

The Art-chetypes project:

I recently tested this system of archetypes with a reportage I did at the 2014 Miami Art Basel art fair. I went around asking artists, art dealers, curators, and visitors about their personal connection to art. In today's highly capitalized art world, I find it is crucial to remind ourselves what attracted us to art in the first place. I asked random people to select from a chart the first archetype that resonated with them out of the twelve following *Art-chetypes:* the art Warrior, the Art-isan, the art Messenger, the art Queen/King, the art Lover, the art Server, the art Juggler, the art Transformer, the art Scholar, the art Entrepreneur, the art Traveler, and the art Sage. It was encouraging to see how everyone immediately and enthusiastically engaged in the experience. This being said, the art crowd is trained in this type of reflection, so the exercise was easy. It is another challenge to engage folks less familiar with their own artistic ability; this is why a journaling approach is an efficient first step to getting acquainted with one's creativity.

An exercise in creative life management:

This project allows the user to quantify the time and energy necessary for each creative activity. We can test and see, ask and offer, ponder and regroup, and over again. We build our own rhythm. Step by step, we design our cadence of self-discovery and creation.

A global vision at one glance:

The wheel configuration allows for a visualization of all twelve aspects of the entity concerned. The geometric configuration displays the full connections between values, elements, existing projects, or participants involved. At one glance, we can evaluate which value is missing and which one is overriding, prepping the terrain for an equalizing intervention.

Testing the values system with the corporate, a case study:

I tested this system of values with corporate organizations interested in restructuring their brand. A Northwest-based American children's clothing company, for example, asked me for advice. The brand was the reference object placed in the center. I presented a first brand restructuring proposition to a team of fifty members. Then, with my help, a selected team of fifteen members responsible for key divisions of the company customized the wheel of twelve values to fit the brand's background, essence, and goals. Product design, marketing, visual merchandising, communication, and web development were actively engaged. This matrix served as a guiding frame throughout the entire duration of the process. Words were defined and visuals were created for external communication of the brand, and strategies were devised according to the values system. It took less than three months to give the kid's wear brand an image makeover that is more contemporary and appealing to modern parents. The wheel structure helped the company to focus and crystallize their ideas, when they weren't sure where to start.

Incubator and frame, the system is a double-purpose container:

Confusion reigns when we don't know where to begin. For a team, restructuring can appear as an insurmountable challenge because there are many moving parts; a jump-start is needed. This system offers a base to build a dialogue. It becomes a foundation rooted in sound values for the elaboration of projects. It acts as an incubator.

But it also serves as a mold strong enough to withstand contradiction, when conflicting ideas from all boards start fusing, when the argument is passionate, when parties with various cultural backgrounds and different missions within the organization don't speak the same language to settle on a strategy acceptable to all.

The same methodology applies for an individual trying to achieve reconciliation between the clashing parts within the self.

A detailed description used for refinement:

This tool is used for self-definition. It encourages the user to fill out the blanks in the twelve categories on the wheel and tweak the terminology used to describe values at discretion. The use of synonyms helps us enrich descriptions of the self or of projects.

I am personally testing these archetypal energies and numbers as I apply their directions to write this book. Each chapter builds layers of characteristics inherent to the energy of its matching number and archetype, in an effort to reveal more of the future physical manifestations of this project.

It forces me to narrow down the concept with greater precision. It gives me the words and references I need to feel confident and explain my idea to potential collaborative parties. If the active principle of this tool works for me, it could be of use to others as well.

Deepening the process:

This wheel of values can be utilized at several levels. We can use it repeatedly to further investigate a given idea. Once the user has worked a first time through the twelve-step circuit and delineated the ballpark of a concept, he or she can take a second turn at the wheel of values to sharpen definitions, then a third turn, and so on.

In a way, our wheel multiplies through this progression; it morphs from one basic flat two-dimensional program into a *spiral* made of layers of wheels. Each new wheel gives refined information that shines light on the project at a slightly different angle, accentuating or eclipsing elements, and bringing perspective to the original rendering. The flat wheel unfurls into a three-dimensional coil as we question further, metaphorically conferring depth to its meaning.

I can choose a platform design that displays a perspective effect in order to render the depth of the analytical process.

Our screen experience is flat; it would be more attractive and real with dimension and space.

A web of concentric wheels:

Another way to use the wheel is to confront different projects. An entity could start applying the wheel of values to its brand identity, but also to product development, and to a particular division of the company, and confront these three wheels to check if all values are matched.

A quantity of concentric wheels can be obtained, all pertaining to the same brand, operating in a circular way around the center goal of improvement, with the twelve values acting as intersection points and common denominators.

The magic behind spirals:

Humanity has been fascinated with spirals since the Neolithic period. These powerful symbols are depicted in many forms of ancient culture all over the planet.[82] To my sense, they are no less than a continuous representation of the numerous tripartite symbols and pictograms that we discussed in chapter 3.

A spiral is a vortex through which we dive into the rabbit hole of our own mysteries, from which we wind into self-discovery and wind out in exploration of the external world. The spiral, like a Kundalini[83] fire, is the geometric figure that allows a continuous, non-broken movement, smoothly adding dimension to our existence. Just as the double helix of human DNA represents the essence of our life, the spiral symbolizes the ineluctable progress of physical reality. The spiral permits safe ascension without disruption.

It can act as a corkscrew to extract what no longer serves us. In this case, it becomes a tool for cleansing and healing, ultimately for the purpose of self-realization. It can also act as a drill to surgically drive new elements into our experience.

Templates for a customized values system:

This frame of values will be tweaked to the desired requirements in any categories of interest, topic, or place. It can be tailored to anyone's lifestyle, age, culture, location, or social background. These frames are templates.

For instance, we can create a wheel for company divisions, where values are affiliated to different divisions of the same company. For instance the fourth, fifth, and sixth values of management, art, and service could respectively represent the divisions of human resources, design, and marketing. It is up to each company to decide which division matches which value according to their brand's essence, and build templates accordingly.

We can create templates for colors, geometric shapes, or locations, each with twelve categories matching the characteristics of each value.

Templates can be tweaked at will and customized to the user's requirements. Adjustability is required for this tool, because parameters will be modified as the user journals on the platform and grows creatively.

A crowd-induced process:

The quantity of possible templates is unlimited, as they can be applied to events, opportunities, physical objects, concepts, or even more future applications that will make themselves known as the need arises.

It would be interesting to enroll experienced professionals in various business categories, each with the specific language and culture inherent to their expertise, to create templates. "Tweaking teams" can tailor the system of values and design templates in the categories of human resources, design, technology, programming, retail, hosting, finance, manufacturing, and many more. These crowd-generated templates would constitute the beginning of a database of guiding frames that can be used by all on the network.

We need a disciplined system in our Hall of SERVICE.

This is a STRUCTURE.

The sixth set of values calls for a tool to allow for the elaboration of templates according to various categories of business, division, etc.

Multiple wheels inherent to multiple projects that can be filed under one user's profile.

This application shows an architecture of communicating layers.

Analytical, disciplined, and structured, the psychological archetype matching this part of our personality is THE SERVER.

7

BALANCE

Assimilating Our Creative Paradoxes

Co-creation, Interaction, Harmonization, Fairness

In this seventh chapter, the chapter of harmonization, I am interested in exploring the concept of balance. Like the equinox in September, which equalizes the duration of night and day, like a juggler of opposites, we search for a happy medium between circumstances.

On our wheel journey, this is where we dare to venture out and communicate our creativity to our environment.

Interactivity is a feature embedded in humanity:

No human is an island. No matter how hermetic it claims its borders to be, there is no nation immune to its neighbors' strife. Information flows, goods circulate. Borders are an illusion. Nature ignores man's made-up frontiers.

Chief Oren Lyons, a Native faithkeeper from the Onondaga Nation in New York state, addressed delegates at the United Nations in 1992, warning about a global environmental crisis:

> There are some specific issues I must bring forward on behalf of our Nations and Peoples in North America. The issue of nuclear and toxic waste dumps on our precious lands; the policy of finding a place for the waste with the poorest and most defenseless of peoples today. This brings the issue of the degradation of our environment by these waste dumps, over-fishing, over-cutting of timber, and toxic chemicals from mining processes throughout our lands.[84]

As imagined in M. Night Shyamalan's 2004 science fiction movie *The Village*,[85] isolationism is a fantasy induced by fear. Resistance is futile; at a collective level, humanity already chose exchange, the cornerstone of learning and progress.

Step by step, we balance our act and get our inner Robinson Crusoe and inner Citizen Kane to play nice together.

Balance is a universal law of physics:

An empty space is inviting. The universe organically tries to fill in the void. A crack in the earth calls for water and dust. A pond filled to the brim overflows onto neighboring lands. Extremes attract each other. Plus attracts minus, creating movement. The incessant give and take of offer and demand creates flux in our markets, in our physics, and in our emotional states. It also erodes boundaries; with friction and time, the pendulum oscillating between antipodes loses its amplitude and tends to settle in the middle, where it gets faster and faster, until it slows down and finally stops, allowing for peace and re-assessment. That is, if nothing gets in the way.

Balance, really?

Truth is, we don't care much for immobility on this earth plane. We don't like to be stationary for too long. Silence and moderation bore us. We are fervent beings ready to march on and learn from the multitude of potentials available to us. Out of boredom and a lack of sense of purpose, we are known for creating all sorts of dramas to experience intensity and to test our ability to overcome havoc. Even though we know that moderation is wise, we call it average, mediocre. We want more. British philosopher Bertrand Russell even describes envy as: "[o]ne of the most universal and deep-seated of human passions. [...] Envy is the basis for democracy. Heraclitus asserts that the citizens of Ephesus ought all to be hanged because they said, 'There shall be none first amongst us.' The democratic movement in Greek States must have been almost wholly inspired by this passion."[86]

We save the notion of perfect balance for the after life. At this day and hour of flexibility, rigor mortis shows no appeal. We are not here to stand still, we are here to welcome hindrance and create pathways to conquer resistance. We are interns of the real world, eager to ask questions, formulate answers, learn, and do it again. We spurn complacency and build hurdles to keep us on our tip-toes. We get clumsy, as some of our creations get out of hand and turn criminal.

No wonder our economic markets swing between crisis and booms, between over-spending and cutting expenses. No wonder we drone-bomb, we gang rape, we waterboard and we hate such atrocities. No wonder we make political partisanship an axiom, simplistically pitching one side against the other, and we suffer from it. We raise amounts of money that could feed entire countries to outweigh our opponents on the ballot of electoral campaign battles, and we find it obscene. We cover our eyes, oblivious to another's misery. We feel guilty and our hearts break in front of inequality, injustice, violence, poverty. We give to charities and buy ourselves a conscience.

We build up our economic and emotional depressions. We feed tragedy for our own trials and entertainment. In the Hindu scriptures, we are fighting our own monsters; the Mahabharata tells of humanity traversing four ages, or *yugas,* that see the progressive loss of virtues:

> In the Krita age, everything was free from deceit and guile, avarice and covetousness. Virtue like a bull was among men with four legs complete. In the Treta, sin took away one of its legs and virtue had then (only) three legs. In the Dwapara, sin and virtue are mixed half and half. In the dark (Kali) age, virtue, being mixed with three parts of sin, lives by the side of men. Accordingly virtue is said to wait upon men with only a fourth part remaining.[87]

We are out on a limb here. The drive for human expansion is a treasure and a curse. Balance is our paradox.

The attempts at harmonization:

We argued and came up with complex solutions to uproot excess. We tried to empower the poor but leveled the masses disappointingly low; we tried to empower the rich, and we got an even wider divide between social classes; we tried to regulate markets, and created inevitable restrictions that smothered our freedom to create. Globalization opened doors, but devoured local producers and starved small businesses. The development of technology brought us fast communication and education, but automation suppressed many jobs that the middle class survived on. We put a Band-Aid at the top of the iceberg of our deep issues, seeing, hearing, and speaking no evil.

We lived an eternal pull and push in search for harmony within our *physical* world. We are due for an ineluctable *spiritual* harmonizing process.

The original *sin*-drome of imbalance:

Our greed outweighs our values. We are addicted to the physical world, and oblivious of spiritual matters. Our analytical and logical left brain is on overdrive, and our intuitive and creative right brain is atrophied. Our priorities are off. The overcrowded space of materiality leaves no room for newness; it is overfed while the deserted realm of values starves.

Extreme materialism brings greed, while extreme concern with spiritual matters results in detachment from reality. Lucifer, from Latin *light bearing,* is cited once in the King James Bible translation of Isaiah as "shining one, morning star, Lucifer" (Isaiah, 14:12). St. Thomas Aquinas presents the devil as a figure of envy and pride, "is not a fornicator nor a drunkard nor anything of the like sort, yet he is proud and envious."[88] Enochic and Islamic views see Lucifer as an enlightened being refusing to bow before Adam, which can be interpreted as a denial of man and materiality. Striving to stay in the realm of the immaterial, he falls from grace, and is sent to a hell of extreme materialism, a training place to accept the vicissitudes of physical form. The devil is a snob. Seeking bliss within abstraction is just as egotistical as delighting in material goods, and just as incomplete. Matter and spirit are two sides of the same coin of human self-completion.

The other is a mirror:

As discussed in chapter 6, our wheel of twelve numbers is comprised of two equivalent chunks of six entities that mirror each other in symmetry. The astrological wheel places the seventh sign of Libra across its Aries individualistic counterpart, activating the dance with another being.

Along my third journey with the halucinogenic drug ayahuasca, I imagined the yellow sun disk splitting in two half-disks in the complementary colors of orange and violet, and reuniting in its integral original circle, all the while engaging in an energetic conversation with its surroundings. I interpreted it as a choice offered to the human psyche to act either as a whole or as a multiple of itself.

The number 7, coupled with the balancing energy of the constellation of the Scales (Libra), engages us in a doublet with someone else, who is no less than the self in a different outfit. The interaction with another is an invitation to self-recognition, where partners reflect back at each other selected aspects of their personas. Our best friend impersonates our inner beauty, while our worst enemy incarnates what we hate most about ourselves.

I faced a catch-22 situation when I was asked whether this material was geared toward individuals or groups: both aspects are ultimately one and the same, as teamwork starts within the self. Introspection and team binding are close disciplines.

Temperance, an intention to balance spirit and matter:

This seventh aspect brings about a dance of reflections that is a key engine in self-development but also in successful teamwork, offering chances to smooth out opinions and invite spirit in the material world. In the mystical Tarot, this aspect is impersonated by the major Arcanum The Temperance, interestingly the fourteenth (2 x 7) major Arcanum located between major Arcana number thirteen and number fifteen, respectively Death and The Devil. These intense two cards carry the energy of opportunities and transmutation (Death card),[89] and acknowledgment of one's addictions (Devil card).[90] The Temperance[91] is a figure pouring liquid from one cup to the other as an attempt to equalize its opposites.

The conciliating power in paradox:

We can hold opposite points of view and entertain peaceful debates at once, as demonstrated by St.Thomas Aquinas' colossal effort in his *Summa Theologica* to expose a synthesis of philosophy and revelation as complementary instead of antagonistic.

When we have the opportunity to embrace two seemingly opposite concepts, we stand in the middle and entertain both opinions. We establish a bridge between two interlocutors, whether they are distinct people or two facets of the self. Internally, we regenerate ourselves when we assimilate our paradoxes. Like the *Ouroboros*, a snake biting its own tail, we are offered the possibility to connect our contradictions. This balancing act is first and foremost an internal affair. There is no world peace before folks have first achieved peace within; challenge and support are both contained within the seed of paradox.

The unwobbling pivot of justice:

Like the fulcrum between the two plateaus of a scale, our set of values seeks justice. Poet Ezra Pound translates Confucius' *Chung Yung, Doctrine of the Mean*, written in the sixth century B.C., as the *Unwobbling Pivot*:[92]

> Happiness, rage, grief, delight. To be unmoved by these emotions is to stand in the axis, in the center [...]. That axis in the center is the great root of the universe [...] [i]f the country be well governed, he does not alter his way of life from what it had been during the establishment of the regime; when the country is ill governed, he holds firm to the end, even to death, unchanging. His is an admirable rectificative energy.[93]

The sword of harmony aims at sincerity, cuts through illusions, and brings clarity.

Steering away from war:

Fighting slows us down and wastes our time. Bloodsheds leave indelible stains on the lineage of humanity that diplomacy cannot make up for. We learned our lessons in combat and we are now losing interest. We want to devote our time to creating instead. Creation is possible when folks gather under a communal roof and focus first on what they share, while leaving their differences at the door. Debate emerges soon enough, and doubt brings about creativity.

On our wise authority, the system of values becomes a permission slip to start communicating, opening a door for durable creation.

Handing the talking stick over:

It is at the source of impartiality that the clock can be reset, where all parties involved, physical and non-physical, are still gathered in the vessel of common interest. Before imbalance takes place, before hearts are inflamed, a philosophical approach offers bipartisanship. The fence opens to a peace zone in which we can discuss our values. When humanity is in conflict with its own, values offer a land of wisdom in which we can identify the ties between the mundane and our spirituality. We invite discussion to the table, holding all angles in our hearts without stomping on convictions. We allow for settlement with win/win solutions.

Elastic movements:

The speed of modernity is forcing us to stretch beyond our comfort zone. More than ever, adaptability is the recipe for survival. Elasticity is a keyword for business: today suppliers request flexibility from their strategy tools to adjust to the fluctuating demands of their customers. Manufacturing and distribution can reduce or accrue product delivery capacity according to their buyers' seasonal needs. Utilities can be provided on the global service grid according to peak usage. Elastic cloud computing is a popular neologism to describe the processing of electronic data in function of market demand,[94] and a sure recipe for satisfied clients.

Versatility allows us to switch seats, put ourselves in another's shoes, and begin the process of consensus. When we stretch our hearts open to encompass more data, we give ourselves more bandwidth to exercise our free will.

Sharing is what gives us the true experience of creation:

In Buddhism as in the precepts of alchemy, spiritual maturity is reached when lessons from the spirit are applied not only to the self, but also extended to the benefit of other people.

When two people interact, a private dance takes place where each party elicits a unique version of each other. They co-create one another and mutually validate their existence. It is when co-creation is acknowledged and shared that we make it real. It asks for a show-room and a network.

Our proposed platform wants to give shelf space to our superb creations. It offers a way to display and communicate our creativity.

We co-create our world and history:

We engineer our life and we influence the life of others through our deeds based on mental choice and intent. We regiment our environment to minutia. Seen from a higher vantage point, the incredibly detailed infrastructure that bonds collective thoughts, emotions, and facts is interactive, fluid, and fast.

The least of flutters in this gigantic mechanism can have significant implications on the life of many and alter the course of history. We live an interesting contradiction where we are the masters of our providence, yet all is in constant flux influenced by the global mind; we are creating history as we live it. We design our future with our many choices every fraction of a second.

We are readying ourselves to hold this complexity: We have created the internet as a gathering tool to watch what the global community is up to. We are learning to know each other's intentions better. Our crowd movements illustrate a global surrendering to the idea that everything is co-created. This is why this project is keen on surrendering to the global creation. Everyone holds a piece of heaven on earth and has a say in the future of humanity.

Co-resolution:

While working in the field of trend analysis, I particularly enjoyed watching which signals emerge from the collective intent, at what particular moment they reach critical mass, break out to the public's attention, and what the impacts are on consumers' attitudes.

Underneath a trend signal lies a topic that is relevant to large amounts of people and that is eager to be revealed. Trends are whistle-blowers with two possible missions: to help propagate useful ideas, and to allow the release of general afflictions. A mobile phone application that is newly marketed wants to be promoted. But also, a trend for honey in the food category, in beauty formulas, and honey colors in fashion and design, can be an alarm signaling the disappearance of bees; it must surface in order to be seen, denounced, and empathized with. The community decides when the moment is best, once enough exposure and momentum gives it a chance to be embraced and healed.

We co-generate the trend mechanism to divulge what deserves our consideration at a particular moment. Trends are problem-solvers and a form of collective advertisement.

The wheels invite us to expose ourselves to disturbance in a way that we regulate. It is a controlled environment where we can adjust the influx of foreign elements, to give our creative raw material the possibility to be reworked into a new shape. It is a tool to be used in case of conflict to review the pros and cons of a project; it is a solution finder.

The movement generated between void and saturation is eponymous of life. The fundamental force between extremes generates traction or repulsion, then flow and change; life is change. We are kinetic beings. Impermanence is the rule of physical reality. Disturbance is a beautiful incitation to dance; never erased, it seeks to be transformed.

We need balance in our Hall of PARTNERSHIPS.

This is a MOVEMENT.

The seventh set of values calls for interaction between users.

A messaging system is embedded into the digital platform.

Open-minded, pondering, and seeking harmony, the psychological archetype matching this part of our personality is THE JUGGLER.

8

TRANSFORM

TRANSMUTING OUR MYSTERIES

RESPONSIBILITY, DARKNESS, POWER, MYSTICISM

Taking responsibility for free will:

The blame game is an affliction and Western civilization is riding on denial. In the Garden of Eden, Adam refutes responsibility for eating the forbidden fruit and blames Eve for tempting him, while Eve blames the serpent for making her eat it in the first place. My guess is that if they didn't have an appetite for the apple to begin with, they wouldn't have taken it home. By nature, our free will presents us with the choice to consume the fruit on the tree of knowledge of Good and Evil. Ashamed of our original state of nudity, cast from purity and innocence, we embrace duality and separation, and part ways from unity and God.

Blaming is a pretext and a form of self-denial. We became self-haters. Under-exercised, our hearts became somewhat useless; we reduced our identities to the two poles of body and mind. We forgot.

When we wish to set our spiritual identity back to its origination, we hug our drama, we claim our suffering, and we let go of blame in this convenient global amnesia. We take responsibility for free will, for it is the attribute of humanity that we allow no higher power to tamper with, and which is a starting block for our creativity. Creativity *is* free will.

Taking responsibility for our shadows:

There is (r)evolutionary potential in taking full accountability for our giant ecosystem of thoughts, feelings, and acts, for the holy trinity of mind, body, and soul. Individual responsibility can alter consciousness fast and at planetary scale.

What we see in another reflects what is already present inside of us. It takes one to see one. Every piece of news, every demand, every remark thrown at us, every single object that we lay our eyes on, is a response to our personal invitation.

We are given the opportunity to own it. Responsibility is ownership. When an experience belongs to us, we have the power to transform it or disown it.

The particles of emotional dark matter are dense and heavy; their gravitational pull sucks in every beam of light that comes near and traps it.

A high concentration of this tar-like material creates powerful emotional black holes where traction, resistance, and friction build up with such furor that they will only lash out with more violence once freed—if they don't end up turning against themselves and self-destruct. Dark pockets amassed within one's psyche result in illness, rage, despair, self-hatred, or madness. Within a group, those heavy particles pitch brothers against one another and take the shape of ghettos, civil wars, and other conflicts around the world. Yet, we invite the dark matter present in another to act as a mirror to reflect back to us the presence of undigested debris within, so that we can look at it, make it our own, amend it, and free ourselves from it. Turning our back to these particles, we turn off the switch and we empower them, for they feed off denial; they thrive in obscurity. In facing them, we illuminate the room and we gain the ability to dissolve them. Once embraced, they are radiated with light and disintegrated, for light is a form of love. Taking responsibility is a gesture of love.

The mechanism of awareness:

In order to work on something, be it light or dark, we need to bring it to the forefront of our attention. Consider this software analogy: We cannot edit the digital layer of a document unless it is on the forefront of our screen page; the computer application won't let us treat what is not highlighted. The same goes with mind configuration. We have to bring elements into the spotlight of our perception where we can see them and work on them.

Un-learning obsolete beliefs:

Sufi mystic Hazrat Inayat Khan is believed to have said: "There can be no rebirth without a dark night of the soul, a total annihilation of all that you believed in and thought that you were."[95] Going through this calcination process brings light in dark areas of the self, to help us to un-learn what hampers us.

For years I suffered hip pain from a repetitive sports injury. It was finally cured by chiropractors using methods that temporarily deprogram harmful memorized nervous reflexes between the brain and the body. The energetic circuitry of the body can be restored to its original healthful settings through acupressure or manipulation before chiropractic adjustment. One practitioner would have me lie on my stomach and move my leg sideways and up, in a vigorous circular alternate motions. This unnatural movement was foreign to my body and was meant to "confuse the brain" right before a final swift adjustment was keyed in. It felt strange, scary, and painless, and over repeated sessions the pain went away.

Our core fear is a deep buried treasure:

We can deprogram the belief embedded into our genes for generations that we are doomed to succumb to separation, fear, or violence. We no longer need to learn our earth lessons through trauma. Those are programmed in our global memory and will always exist, as long as we choose to feed them and replicate them in our energy field once we identify them. As Ihaleakala Hew Len, Ph.D., a practitioner of the Hawaiian healing technique of Ho'oponopono asserts, "We have put a mortgage on our soul." This ancient practice in reconciliation and forgiveness consists in encircling our issues with the four-sided mantra "I'm sorry, please forgive me, I love you, thank you". Our memory can be wiped clean of rubble once we take responsibility for it.[96] When this loaded database is released, fact after fact, person after person, we have the honest choice to explore darkness on account of our own free will.

Darkness for the mainstream:

In my experience, the eighth value of darkness and transformation is not the easiest one to discuss in a creative session in a traditional work environment; darkness is often associated with death or destruction and marketers discard it as a scarecrow for the main consumer.

Death disturbs us, even when presented as the end of a cycle, precursory to rebirth. Transformation is a form of death before re-creation, and we are reluctant to investigate its benefits, especially when it leads us to introspection. Yet we owe darkness a visit.

Darkness wants to regain its *titre de noblesse*:

Dark is beautiful. Dark is what is yet to come. It bears the unknown, and our mind is thrilled by a good enigma. Its existence simply allows our intelligence to do its job of questioning and seeking answers. Mystery is the reason for the mind to be alive. The darker the secret, the shrewder the debunking, the smarter the solutions we can find. The mind is a clever detective and a brilliant resolver. We build charades to train our skills and broaden our knowledge. Darkness is a fertile vessel for the mechanism of intellectual understanding.

Khem is the name of the dark alluvium from the Nile delta that gave its name to the land of Egypt in the Old Kingdom: *Kmt*, or Black Land. In hieroglyphic translation, *-khem* is a suffix indicating termination, or the color black. Etymologically, the word *khem* is the root of the words *alchemy* and *chemistry*.[97]

Darkness asks to be reinstated. It has been vandalized and it wants to clear its name. Darkness is the indicator for light and its instrument of gradation; it is the fecund soil for our personal and collective memories that offers an opportunity to strengthen our emotional body and make us whole.

Commercial darks:

In mainstream fashion in the United States, dark can be a hard sell beyond the formal black outfits we know, largely inspired by the iconic little black dress popularized by Coco Chanel and Jean Patou in the 1920s.[98] In the beauty arena too, dark cosmetics for a street consumer are more easily appreciated when associated with evening wear and entertainment rather than with transformation. Yet there is much to play with in these opaque, liquid, mysterious, and troubling effects. Luxury brands love an intense dark look, and it is a favorite among creative team members who are exposed to the newest trends.

Juniors and the dark:

The gothic look seduces junior brands. Eventually the youth, with its fascination for all things vampire, zombie, tattoos, and piercings, might vanquish the old ghost and give darkness a good rap. I remember seeing youth in the country of Bhutan, a safe place of traditional lifestyles in my experience, watching DVDs of horror movies in the back alleys of a market with great fascination. I saw a large number of T-shirts in clothing lines with printed skulls, death symbols, and the faces of troubled pop stars such as Kurt Cobain, Jimmy Hendrix, or Jim Morrison. Quite an antagonistic attitude to the Gross National Happiness policy described in chapter 4. After all, it's a natural reaction to get bored with goodness and want to explore our demons when we get too comfortable.

Darkness is wild and female:

The first image that comes to mind when the idea of darkness is brought up at a fashion ideation table in the U.S. is Halloween—a lightweight expression for such a powerful myth, too quick to divert the subject. Sorcery is a profound concept; it has been used by mankind to burn away its core fear of the inner mysteries of the human psyche. Darkness is associated with internalization, a trait that the female body symbolizes. Women have been oppressed and exploited for the longest time.

The repression of the Female Principle:

The United Nations blog on global issues states sad facts:

> Every year, millions of women and girls worldwide suffer violence, be it domestic violence, rape, female genital mutilation/ cutting, dowry-related killing, trafficking, sexual violence in

conflict-related situations, or other manifestations of abuse. [...] Women and girls who experience violence suffer a range of health problems and their ability to participate in public life is diminished. Violence against women harms families and communities across generations and reinforces other violence prevalent in society.[99]

The repression of the feminine through the oppression of women affects all of society. The resulting wounded spawn has colossal effects on the global psyche. Bringing mass awareness to this issue will help to change traditions and mentalities toward gender, as will electing more women to positions of power worldwide.

Female guidance:

Some feminists question the very notions of sex and gender; gender theorist Judith Butler poses that they are socially constructed[100] and claims that "behavior creates your gender."[101] Other feminists, such as ethicist Carol Gilligan, agree that fundamental ethical differences exist between the feminine and the masculine voices: "Since masculinity is defined through separation while femininity is defined through attachment, male gender identity is threatened by intimacy while female gender identity is threatened by separation."[102]

Education philosopher Nel Noddings shares this view in her work *Caring: A Feminine Approach to Ethics and Moral Education*.[103]

The Female Principle is one of creation, spiritual nurturing, and psychological fulfillment that becomes distorted when it tries to please a male-dominated society.

Clarissa Pinkola Estés is an American poet, psychoanalyst, and post-trauma specialist of ethnic heritage who has written extensively about the Wild Woman archetype. She wonders: "So why [...] do women try to bend and fold themselves into shapes that are not theirs? I must say, from years of clinical observation of this problem, that most of the time it is not because of deep-seated masochism or malignant dedication to self-destruction or anything of that nature. More often it is because the woman simply doesn't know any better. She is unmothered."[104]

The feminine attribute is everybody's concern:

These considerations on the feminine and the masculine sides of the psyche affect men and women alike. All of us host male and female aspects, regardless of our gender.

Jungian psychologist Marion Woodman wisely states: "The word 'feminine,' as I understand it, has very little to do with gender, nor is woman the custodian of femininity. Both men and women are searching for their pregnant virgin. She is the part of us who is outcast, the part who comes to consciousness through going into darkness, mining our leaden darkness, until we bring her silver out."[105]

The pregnant virgin within:

Marion Woodman sees as virginal the creative power used to define one's identity. We are still new and shy at this. When we develop intimacy with our core, we no longer try to be another. We are able to see our naked truth. Blocks are released, pretense falls away. Prodigal daughters of transformation, we re-enter triumphant the gates of Eden. Dauntlessly, we claim motherhood over our creations.

We make peace with the witch and the druid within; we make space for our wizardry.

I would like this project to incite users to embrace the feminine part of their identity and to challenge them to check out the unknown; in exploring unfamiliar categories of interests, they can unlock doors to their own riddles. In trying themselves at activities they have never tackled before or are uneasy with, they can awaken undiscovered passions. We will discuss further the key concept of intimacy in chapter 12.

Online shadows and transparency:

Security is a major basic need; it corresponds to our first chakra, the seat of our fight-or-flight response, the root, the foundation upon which the second chakra of creativity lays.

There are co-created skeletons in the closet of the internet and safety is key. We can't see the many faces at work in the shadows of the fiber optics. Cyberfraud and cyberbullies are a global concern. Transparency, Hazrat Inayat Khan's "all-pervading-light suffusing the Cosmos,"[106] is called in for clearance. The world wants disclosure on governance, pointing at dubious trade secrets. We track spies or investigate concealed corporate ownerships that pull the strings of markets, in order to expose and neutralize harmful manipulation. Citizens want to know where profit goes and what happens with taxpayers' money. Consumer defense organizations denounce companies selling big data on the back of buyers and online users. When we globally treat ourselves as products, we become human traffickers in the big cathouse of the web.

Privacy versus secrecy:

Users demand to know how personal data is handled on the network, with no deliberate selling of private information to third parties. Our projected digital platform wants to offer a level of privacy where users can experiment with their own wheel until it is ready to be exposed to the cyber public in three levels of privacy: total (access reserved strictly to the user), partial (groups), or nonexistent (public).

Our creativity asks to be shielded from paparazzi. There are thieves out there prying to loot great ideas. Our private life needs discretion to avoid being discriminated against. A person with particular background, tastes, looks, health or finance records asks for a tabula rasa to start fresh relationships and endeavors.

However, secrecy doesn't serve the purpose of anti-discrimination in the long haul; it deflects it and builds it up instead. Once again, drama feeds off resistance and secrecy is a form of resistance. Discrimination will be eradicated when people's stories are divulged, digested, and accepted by the crowd. The first victims are sacrificial lambs tearing down the barriers of intolerance. Most of us do not want to play this role consciously; neither do we want our loved ones to assume it. But some souls commit to losing their health, time, energy, money, hope, and even their lives, in a battle against thorny causes. People in history will be remembered for their heroism in standing firm in the face of disdain, hatred, rejection, and violence, and we can be grateful to the likes of Rosa Parks, Harvey Milk, Ron Woodroof, Aung San Suu Kyi, Malala Yousafzai, and all soldiers who took arms against intolerance, altering minds and behaviors in our communities for the better.

Healing through creativity:

In the context of spiritual awakening, "healing retreats" are promoted. Many of us believe that we need soul therapy; but are we really sick? In a way we are: at a global and personal level, much needs to be released and removed. Destructivity, just like creativity, is an art. Yet some of us with pure intentions are dabbling in doubt and as a result are trifling with compromise. Like Clarissa Pinkola Estés's unmothered beings, we are diverted in unfulfilling activities and we lose our heart along the way. Creative focus follows Darwin's law of evolution: it promotes the survival of the fittest, phasing out what no longer works for us and relegating less favored actions to the end of our list of priorities. Focusing on what we are the most passionate about will bring us automatically to a state of being where there is nothing left to heal.

Creative therapy:

The enigmatic thirteenth zodiacal sign, Serpentarius, sometimes recognized by Western astrology, corresponds to the constellation of Ophiuchus. It was identified by Claudius Ptolemaeus in the second century B.C. and is located between the constellations of Scorpius (affiliated in Western astrology to the zodiacal sign of Scorpio) to the west and Sagittarius to the east. Like the Ouroboros, it is depicted by a serpent that not only merges its opposites but also is a powerful symbol of death and rebirth, a cosmic pattern in the Hindu, Aztec, or Egyptian cultures. It is a myth of resurrection in Christian tradition (I Kings, 17; Job, 14) as well, or a symbol of psychic liberation in Siberian shamanism or Zen Buddhism with the teachings on the identity of life and death.[107] The snake is a representation of the healing spiral with its coiling serpent(s) in the shape of the caduceus, the symbol of medicine.[108]

Healing is an automatic corollary of our fertile and creative pursuits. Creativity *is* the therapy.

This platform's design will allow people to be exposed to foreign ideas close enough to ring a bell, but far enough to act as an intruder; close enough to stimulate, and far enough to harm. Close enough to nurture, and far enough to lose focus.

The proposed journaling activity will lead us through a personal initiatory journey on the lemniscate of the number 8, where we can be our own psychopomp and find our way to the place of our soul. We can jump through the ring of fire to lead ourselves and our teams through catharsis.

The platform is a safe room for self-discovery.

We need a laboratory to explore in our Hall of TRANSFORMATION.

This is an EXPERIMENT.

The eighth value calls for a private space where one can face personal secrets.

This application is our own Pandora's box, where we take responsibility for our life's events and treat them as stimulating experiences with transformative power to stimulate our creativity.

Deep, inquisitive, and a daredevil, the psychological archetype matching this part of our personality is THE TRANSFORMER.

9

KNOW

INVITING GLOBAL CULTURE INTO OUR CREATIVE VISION

PHILOSOPHY, EDUCATION, EXPLORATION, STORYTELLING

Values as personal advisors:

The number 9 is the number associated with completion. In the base 9 numeral system,[109] in which digits of large numbers are added to each other until reduction to a single digit, 9 is the neutral number that never affects the result of an addition. Symbolically, its energy is impartial, solid, and open.

In Western astrology, the ninth zodiac constellation is Sagittarius, the Centaur half-horse half-man holding his bow. The archer aims at and meets the target. This allegory stands for knowledge, philosophy, education, and travel.

This project is inspired by ancient knowledge. So are the chapters of this material. Who doesn't approve of the virtues of truth, justice, or honesty? These words have been motivating humanity for over 4,500 years. They are so revered that they make crowds weep when declaimed by a charismatic leader. Transformation and innovation are enduring laws of nature and they become values. So do knowledge, service, and collaboration, venerated commandments in the business world. These principles have the power to federate instead of separate us. They form a basis of communication, a language that conjures up the spell of global misunderstanding, cause for discord as in the biblical tale of the Tower of Babel: "Therefore was the name called Babel; because the LORD did there confound the language of all the earth; and from thence did the LORD scatter them abroad upon the face of all the earth [Genesis 11:9]."[110]

We prepare the terrain to accept different beliefs, to exchange considerations, and thereby to expand our playing field for creativity.

Whether this project takes the shape of a web tool, a software, a methodology, a bank of data, or a community, it always asks these overarching values to infuse everything we do and to wink at us like old friends. They sit next to us as wise advisors when we seek inner guidance.

They are keepers, replacing the gurus and spiritual interpreters of the old days who have become unfit to guide us.

Religion and manipulation:

Our organized religious groups are the go-to guys for those of us disconnected from our ability to discern. They provide us with a sense of belonging, spiritual comfort, and a structure for morality and justice. They are the crutch without which many of us without anchors would spin out of control. Some cults ban the one who strays from sameness; they are known to deliver truths that are deviant versions of ancient texts, either through dubious translations of extinct languages or extraction of excerpts placed out of context. After all, the etymology of the word religion is *religare,* Latin for *to bind; religio* is Latin for *obligation, bond, reverence.* The problem starts there: bond often leads to domination.

Being religious to oneself:

Manipulation through religion is still a common occurrence today. The distortion is not necessarily intentional; most translators are fervent believers of the word they preach. Their sincerity is explanatory of their success. Yet whether intentional or not, the result remains the same. Dogma estranges the unworthy from his own heart, which will only generate more alienation. When we subscribe to dogma, we lose the chance of developing discernment; our critical sense atrophies. We lose communication with our inner wisdom. The true sense of heresy is the forgetfulness of our spiritual inheritance and in my opinion, a crime against the self. If there is one tie that has the power to serve us beautifully, it is the allegiance to oneself. Every individual can reconnect with their divinity in forming their own religion and bond to their personal vows.

We are born pre-formatted with straight access to our inner wisdom. The source of wisdom is within, not without.

Rebranding religion:

Religions are a niche for anthropological research, yet they are endangered unless they get a facelift. Religions have a future when they rebrand themselves with a less binding name, when they empower each individual to sanctify their divinity, without shame, guilt, or fear of punishment.

They will survive when they agree that they are all branches of the same tree, when they focus on the common denominator and promise humanity to itself. In the age of data sharing and open source exchange, ownership over the concept of God is obsolete. Spiritual groups will survive who license women into leading roles in their organizations. Without half of humanity, messages can only be half-messages. It is obvious that there are issues about a woman's experience and body that can only be addressed justly by women.

Self-education to find inner guidance:

By definition, manipulation can only be perpetrated by a more knowledgeable being over another. Education is the antichrist to moral enslavement.

There is much to rediscover in the dialectical methods of critical thinking. Mystical traditions such as Buddhism or Sufism encourage individuals to go out and explore schools of thought to forge their own education. Marcus Aurelius, Roman emperor from 161–180 A.D. and a Stoic philosopher, writes in his *Meditations*:[111]

> Make for thyself a definition or description of the thing which is presented to thee, so as to see distinctly what kind of a thing it is in its substance, in its nudity, in its complete entirety, and tell thyself its proper name, and the names of the things of which it has been compounded, and into which it will be resolved. For nothing is so productive of elevation of mind as to be able to examine methodically and truly every object that is presented to thee in life [...].

Our contemporary self-help books advocating meditation couldn't give us a better recommendation. Ancient texts are treasure chests of information. May every one of us handpick from scriptures the excerpts and translations that resonate best with our personal needs; we can carve out our own values system accordingly. With knowledge, we can restore the umbilical silver cord[112] of communication to the source within, allowing us to receive messages directly from our inner guidance and to keep the channel as clear as possible.

Incorporating humanities into our educative curriculum:

There is a deficiency in the academic curriculum today; students are trained to market themselves in a society driven by consumption. Our view of achievement is filtered through the lens of productivity and sales, and we measure our economic success with Gross Domestic Product quantified by financial gain. We are driven by numbers and science. Without historical and social references, we repeat past errors. Human travails must be told; old is gold. We will benefit from restoring the humanities in our education system. We are concerned that a degree in philosophy or history doesn't pay, and understandably so: the employment situation is globally tough, and private education creates colossal student debts. To repay these loans, young professionals are forced to drink the Kool-Aid and train exclusively for corporate jobs that pay well at entry level, leaving little room for culture and critical thinking. Balance needs to be re-established between marketing and the humanities with hybrid curricula, even if it means to set out on one's own randomized learning journey.

Walking the talk:

In concrete matters, I respect practical experiences as a key companion to theoretical knowledge. "Walking the talk" confers credibility to an entrepreneur. The worker starting his career in production knows the time and effort necessary to complete manual tasks by having performed them repeatedly. She will be respected because she knows about things before she talks about them and gives her instructions.

Curiosity through exploration:

Curiosity is a staple of our education. Access to information is faster and freer; we become knowledge-thirsty globetrotters set on physical and cyber travel. We develop a taste for nomadism and discovery.

I conduct excursions through New York City to educate sales and marketing teams on global culture and trends. We go through the streets to look at various stores, art galleries, or restaurants; we point at colors, designs, or merchandising displays that intrigue us by their newness. We bring to each other's attention peculiar street art and folks with uncommon looks. An analysis is then conducted in brainstorm sessions, followed by strategy exercises relevant for the brand.

Every creative professional performs market analysis. It is second nature to all of us to explore and deduct, even unconsciously, as we stroll about in our everyday lives shopping for food, taking the kids to school, going to the gym, or browsing online. Yet we can improve our observation skills in becoming more aware of them, and we can make it a starting point for a professional analysis.

A comparative tool for observed data:

We can fill out the boxes on our wheel of values with the various elements observed throughout our expeditions as they relate to each particular concept. It will be interesting to crosscheck several trips and single out the busiest values to deduct global directions. The wheel becomes a comparative tool for market analysis.

During my executive years I did a project for a U.S.-based international kitchenware company. We used this system to understand the differences for this type of product between local color trends in France, Japan, Brazil, and the United States. The exploration of each culture, customer habits, and store looks helped me to pinpoint the variations between the different countries and propose a global color card with local accents that was later successfully implemented on the market.

History and education:

We learn considerably from historical periods of expansion, of which the last hundred years are a striking example, for the exponential amount of technological and scientific discoveries that have been made thus far.

We are rekindling an interest in our ancient history. Classical Greece, especially around the fourth century B.C., which saw the development of Plato's Academy, is considered the cultural cradle of Western civilization, and has been referenced profusely in this book. The Renaissance (French for *rebirth*) period is also worthy of mentioning in this chapter on education, discovery, and humanism, because of its impact on global progression.

Renaissance, a story of abundance and diversity:

The opening to science, art, and spirituality concurred with an interest in alchemy and magic, expanding the human spirit.

Starting in the late fourteenth century, Europe entered a period of cultural and commercial expansion. Upon the invention of the printing press, credited to Gutenberg around 1450, and the propagation of paper, education soared. Curiosity and the promise of gain sent explorers and navigators to the Americas, to Africa and to the Far East along the Silk Road. New territories were seized for the ruthless appropriation of riches; colonial empires split the pie of world resources on the basis of first come, first served, demarcating state borders as we still know them today. Yet colonization also made global culture more available: the development of commerce with caravans of exotic merchandise such as spices, fabrics, and fragrances is at the origin of the appearance of a new societal class, with merchants building a bridge between peasantry and nobility. On the art side, sculptors, poets, and painters emerged and so did thinkers with the Humanist movement. Scientists made great progress in astronomy, mathematics, architecture, and biology. Polymath creators were commissioned to research and produce chefs-d'oeuvre of knowledge and aesthetics. Those who approached science with art and spirituality had a chance at being publicized after the obscurantism of the Middle Ages and the systematic and brutal dismissing of any thoughts that challenged clerical authority. From that period, emblematic figures such as Paracelsus, Teresa of Avila, and Leonardo da Vinci contributed to epistemological progress.

Over a period of economic and cultural affluence lasting three centuries, the Renaissance saw an increase in the tolerance toward others' ideals, beliefs, and tastes. Salman Rushdie's novel *The Enchantress of Florence* gives a vivid depiction of interactive communities with different religions and socio-political systems co-existing peacefully, from the Medicis in Florence to the Chinese emperors of the Ming Dynasty, passing by the Indian Moguls, the warlords of Central Asia, and the Ottoman Empire. The book describes in great detail the lifestyles, trades, craftsmanship, ways of transportation, food recipes, clothing styles, and romances of those days. It is a valuable reference for apparel and product designers. I encourage design students to research this period of history and this book in particular, to enrich their personal culture.

When we have food on our plates, with clothing and shelter to keep warm, we grow curious about foreign lifestyles and progressive ideas. Invariably, when resources abound, minds expand. Of course, we must keep in mind the paradox that economic expansion and improvement of society during this time was controversially built on colonialism and slavery.

Educating and motivating through journaling:

Keeping a journal of our journeys is beneficial for us personally as we keep track of our educational process. It helps us to remember facts that we would have forgotten if we hadn't laid them down in writing; it helps us to deduct more consciously the positive effects on our personal evolution; it helps us to refine our values. Once we share those deductions with others, we inspire them in turn as they learn through our experience.

Our digital platform can also include a collective journaling tool where protagonists share their various appreciations of an experience. It is illuminating for each participant to discover the same event seen through a different angle. Some feedback can appear as positive, neutral, or even hurtful, but in any case it will be creative and mind-opening. It will certainly facilitate discussions in a work environment.

Most of our digital platforms let us record a multitude of events, yet they are not structured in a way that helps us to focus on how our various experiences have creatively transformed our life vision and made us progress individually and in our social settings.

From history to storytelling:

I am also inspired by a story from the Book of Revelations in the New Testament.

St. John's vision of the Apocalypse (from Greek *to uncover*) describes the futuristic projection of a version of the city of Jerusalem living in perfect harmony between its people. I am interested in the end passage that portrays the twelve tribes of Israel in relation to the zodiac categories, each with 12,000 sons who built a three-dimensional cubic-shaped city with the following description:

> 21:12. And had a wall great and high, *and* had twelve gates, and at the gates twelve angels, and names written thereon, which are *the names* of the twelve tribes of the children of Israel:
>
> 21:13 On the east three gates, on the north three gates; on the south three gates; and on the west three gates.
>
> 21:14 And the wall of the city had twelve foundations, and in them the names of the twelve apostles of the Lamb.
>
> 21:16. And The city lieth foursquare, and the length is as large as the breadth and the height, twelve thousand furlongs. The length and he breadth and the height of it are equal
>
> 21:17. And he measured the wall thereof, an hundred *and* fourty *and* four cubits, *according* to the measure of a man, that is, of the angel.[113]

Furthermore, in the Water and Tree of Life 22nd verse:

22.2. In the midst of the street of it, and on either side of the river, *was there* the tree of life, which bare twelve *manner* of fruits, *and* yielded her fruit every month: and the leaves of the tree *were* for the healing of the nations."[114]

I find this visionary proposition relevant to our project because it adds a numerological dimension to the astrological, elemental, and cultural description. That's plenty of twelves, threes, and fours to resonate with our project. The mention of a man-angel can also be equated to the archetype of a creative human living in harmony with its surroundings. St. John's New Jerusalem appears as a utopian parable, yet I am interested in exploring how some aspects of its structure could operate on a digital form.

The collective consciousness is an accessible storage room of memories:

Spiritualists such as theosophists and anthroposophists have a concept called the Akashic Records, a giant collective memory where all actions, thoughts, and intentions ever brought into existence are stored. It is a library holding the records of every fact and potential in any area of history.

It would require a mind with monumental memory to consciously contain the totality of this data all at once; it would be the all-seeing eye that illuminates causes and consequences, brings logic and meaning to all acts, facts and artifacts, for those of us interested in learning from our collective history.

I find that we can access those records, at least partially, with faith, will and a persistent practice. We can retrieve information psychically from this global memory when we reach a higher state of awareness. This state of awareness can be achieved through deep meditation or dream-state, in which our brain experience cognitive dreaming, premonitions, or déjà-vus. We can access these records right before we go to sleep, as we find the ability to envision movie-like scenes with vivid images and sounds unfolding in our imagination in hyper- realistic quality.

Since this storage room also holds potentials, it acts as a library of the future.

I am inspired by the concept of a library holding the memory of our creations, and would like our platform to recall and deliver its records under a form of easily accessible broadcasting.

Nomadic and entrepreneurial, a new way to trade:

I participated in a traveling tradeshow that promotes exploration and cross-disciplinary trade called the Retail Design Show ROAD. Professionals in various industries interested in joining forces to hold sales meetings received exposure from and gave exposure to their peers, expanding their clients' lists to a larger circle. Venues were chosen to be larger than offices but more convivial and more central to each town than most convention centers. The first session took place in San Francisco. The various partners rented a contemporary space in an up-and-coming area of town. We outlined a seminar program and set exclusive meetings with each client. We showed our work and networked. I participated in the educational seminar series. It was a success, and since then ROAD has traveled to New York City, Istanbul, and Rio de Janeiro. The nomadic and entrepreneurial characters of this project are a good example of business practices succeeding today: Open, flexible, mobile, design-driven, enthusiastic, and cross-disciplinary. Long live the example of ROAD.

Multiple sources for learning:

Any place is a potential goldmine of information, and any moment is auspicious to our education. Opportunities for knowledge are omnipresent. One can travel as far as the end of the world, or as close as the next block, and learn equally.

Books, magazines, newspapers, blogs, seminars, documentaries, art exhibitions, performances, tradeshows, concerts—any inputs pertaining to global culture—are valid sources of knowledge to analyze where the global mood of consumers is headed. Indubitably, so are movies, television series, and even the popular press.

The elusiveness of history and the validity of popular culture:

History is a collection of stories; it is always subjective, as it is always told through a human voice, *his*-story or *her*-story indeed. Philosopher Michel Foucault notes in his *Archeology of Knowledge* that:

> On the one hand, [the history of ideas] recounts the by-ways and margins of history. Not the history of the sciences, but that of imperfect, ill-based knowledge, which could never in the whole of its long, persistent life, attain the form of scientificity. [...] The history not of literature but of that tangential rumour, that everyday, transient writing that never acquires the status of an oeuvre, or is immediately lost; the analysis of sub-literatures, almanacs, reviews and newspapers, temporary successes, anonymous authors. [...] The analysis of opinions rather than of knowledge, of errors rather than truth [...]. [115]

Countless fleeting facts and anonymous interventions all make history, bringing even more diversity to an already complex compilation of data.

Over-entertainment and decadence:

Entertainment has become a staple of popular culture. Yet it has made us lazy about reflection and debate. We get used to constant noise, to the point of dizziness. Our attention span is short. There is no time allowed for the mind to stay idle and ponder; we don't reevaluate our lives.

The amount of hammering advertising that is force-fed to viewers on television is a nuisance, especially in America. This cheap form of entertainment is numbing and is driving down the level of education of viewers. It makes audiences surreptitiously prone to consuming without questioning the quality of the products advertised. It perpetrates the marketing of useless crap and extends the viability of companies selling things that should be called *bads* instead of *goods*.

Unused cells of our organism degenerate; our minds need a good challenge every now and then to prevent brain decadence and keep the juices of creative stimulation flowing. Advertising could be both entertaining and useful, informative and educational. For networks to ignore this opportunity is almost a crime by omission.

New interpretations of ideas:

Hermeneutics is the branch of knowledge that deals with inter-pretations, originally of biblical and literary texts, and by extension of philosophy and wisdom material. Interpretation of knowledge and analogy are storytelling operations that fuel creativity, entertain the intellect, and boost our memory. Our platform can be enhanced with a software application suggesting new associations in our brain. It informs and stimulates the user.

An educational tool:

Storytelling is the mechanism by which children are taught to remember lessons. A visual description allows for an identification process and an emotional experience. When we make the story our own, we memorize it more easily. We increase our capacity to create.

This platform is a place where we tell our own stories. It can become a catalogue of inspiring diaries.

In time, this platform potentially gathers enough activity to become a storyteller.

It becomes a newsroom to expose projects and give leverage to creative individuals. It can be a channel for creative information, a library of inspirational content available for all to see.

It is only fair to give back to the creative community a return on their initial investment of personal material.

We request a library for our Hall of KNOWLDEGE.

This is a CULTURE.

The ninth value calls for a journaling tool for individuals and for groups to progress and inspire others with their creative evolution.

Curious, knowledgeable, and a great teacher, the psychological archetype matching this part of our personality is THE SCHOLAR.

10

UTILIZE

BUILDING A CREATIVE ENTERPRISE

DURABILITY, MIDDLEMEN,
ENTREPRENEURSHIP, BARTERING

We create the concept of time with our stories:

Time is a construct. We build time lines and time spirals[116] to hold the record of events, each with their specific vibration. A timeline with a matching frequency emitted by another human being will resonate with our own timeline. Storylines with similar and opposite characteristics attract and repel each other like magnets. We invite frequencies into our field and perform a theater act together on the collective clock of earth reality. As in a complex movie entangling layers of lives of strangers, we create meeting points that we call synchronicities. We understand our power to temporize the pace of history. We co-create it. A story unfolding is the manifestation of a time spiral unfurling. We are multidimensional. We jump off strings of time once our energy has shifted and no longer fits into the particular frequency of the story. We shift from script to script when we move location, change jobs, and end relationships, or simply when we alter our emotional state. We recalibrate and jump onto frequencies more adapted to our vibrational state as we grow, in search for new lessons and bliss on the Jacob's ladder of our personal ascension.

The brilliant illusion of time:

The higher our consciousness, the more timelines we can live at once. We become masters of time like Chronos or Saturn, the Old Man and ruler planet of the zodiacal sign of Capricorn.

Our mind creates linear time in order to separate and isolate our experiences, so that we can live through them individually, sequentially, and fully. We learn to navigate time collapses, overlaps and re-laps.

We do and undo the future as we form hypotheses. We do and undo the past as we experience emotions inherent to a memory.

Transforming the past:

In modifying the way we feel about our memories, we re-create our past. There is great therapeutic potential in the acknowledgement of this skill, as we can cleanse the pains of our past experiences as well as those of our ancestors. We can rewrite our story and start over unscripted. Experiments on mice have demonstrated that their memory perception can be "flipped" from fearful to cheerful by stimulating regions of the brain that host memory, in erasing or adding painful and blissful stimuli to imprinted experiences.[117]

In the energy of the number 10, equivalent in base 9 to that of a number 1 (1+0=1), time isn't set in stone. We start over at will.

Durability and authenticity are demanded values:

Time is suspended in the concept of durability. Our longevity as a species depends on the longevity of our environment and our creations. We maintain in order to gain. Brands that craft authentic merchandise with durable materials and long-lasting styles are in high demand.

Brands that market biodegradable products are applauded. Disposable goods in the sectors of energy, electronics, clothing, or construction end up as detritus that might soon only find storage in space, to orbit around Earth and other celestial bodies. Lasting merchandise is needed to remedy the overwhelming problem of garbage that asphyxiates the planet, especially since we have a consumption problem.

Consumed in distortion:

The economy of consumption brings us autonomy, comfort, and ease. It liberates us and empowers us. It makes us creative as we identify needs and invent solutions. We explore further through technology. We live longer thanks to chemistry. Modernity frees us and spoils us. Consumption is delicious. But we don't always know our limits. We create excess and we create in excess. The energy, food, and pharmaceutical lobbies take advantage of our bad habits toward overconsumption and mis-consumption. Semantics apart, consumption is a die-hard addiction. How many more cars or handbags does one really need? Do we seriously want to buy health remedies that are advertised to us with side effect warnings such as nausea, diarrhea, dizziness, or loss of libido? Consuming is a setting by default of our modern belief system. Default indeed, when the game becomes a caricature and turns into a traffic ring between addicted consumers and enabling producers.

Consumer activism presses the corporate world to improve ethical standards:

The *Seventh Generation*, an expression commercially battered, alludes to a policy described in the Great Binding Law, *Gayanashagowa* of the Iroquois Six Nations constitution, a document that may have inspired the Constitution of the United States of America. Its policies take into consideration the impact of present actions on future generations.[118]

This conscious approach is drawn forth today. Customers become educated about ethical ways of producing and distributing merchandise. We look at labels and demand proof of composition and provenance. Our purchases determine the market direction toward environmentally and socially friendly products. Many products are not up to our standards, such as in the food category. The informed crowd who can afford to pay more will opt for healthier food options, preferring to spend on preventative rather than curative health measures. Survey firm Nielsen Corporation reports in January 2015 that "Health-minded global consumers put their money where their mouths are".[119] The discontent with the corporatization of food production/distribution as well as the controversy about genetically modified organisms, among others, stand as witnesses to the growing desire for ethical food worldwide.

Supermarket aisles offering products that no longer fit our standards will be deserted by this category of concerned consumers in favor of local, natural, and ethical markets—and to their profit. We are sensible about labor grades, and brands outsourcing their production in sweatshops are weary of the growing scolding power of consumer activism.

The top and middle layers of society are on duty:

Many people in extreme poverty can barely survive. Folks can only be educated in better consumption once they are able to shop, that is, once their economic situations improve. Whether global economic development is catching up with poverty is questionable; greed and corruption are still rampant despite being seriously exposed as of late. Until things get better, those with buying power are the ones who can shop and vote in favor of the struggling folks. Conscious consuming is up to the top (rich willing) and middle layers of society.

Trade is inherent to us:

We are social animals. Exchange is vital to our survival and our enjoyment. We share moments; we call and respond in vibrant conversations; we give each other life through our interactions. We complement one another with the various sets of skills we possess. We deal goods and services; trade is an innate and vibrant trait of humanity.

Trade is ailing:

We got rich with sales. Trading companies have made a fortune on international transactions, especially from places where labor is inexpensive. But as import/export regulations and currencies exchange rates are readjusted, as factory workers from the emerging world protest for higher wages and as outsourcing countries attempt to bring manufacturing back home, trade runs out of breath. It turns into pure investment with fast cash operations. Financial traders are still getting highly paid, but trade is losing its connection with the tangible value of goods and services.

The sales profession is tired:

The younger generation is hardly interested in developing a career in product sales. During my days in the publishing business, I tried to hire sales representatives but met little enthusiasm. Fashion publishing is more competitive now that brands are shorter on budgets and the marketplace is reaching saturation under the proliferation of consultants and bloggers. In the late '90s, sales of apparel publications were guaranteed. Meetings with customers focused on the volume of transactions, whereas now the question is whether they will buy at all, even with a decent product. Sales jobs demand a lot of energy to set up appointments and prepare pitches, for little results. It is also too dry of a profession for young people, who want to express their creativity and build up curriculum credibility. The sales profession is running out of steam, too. This is a blessing in disguise, because it forces us to reevaluate career paths and bring vision, purpose, and a personal touch into our mundane professional activities.

Redefining the notion of the middleman:

Our mind is in mutation; bombarded with information, it holds larger and more complex data. We learn fast; home-schooled online, we read customers FAQ and case studies, we join chat forums and find answers. We need fewer translators to help us make decisions. We skip the middleman when we can speak and decide for ourselves. This goes for many different fields of our lives. The more spiritual intermediaries we designate to define our ethics, the more estranged we grow from our soul center. With regard to our health, the more doctors we throw between the wisdom of the body and that of the soul, the more twisted the diagnostics, and the more inappropriate the medications. Hierarchy and bureaucracy smother our legislative processes; in a large structure, years can pass between the moment an issue is identified and the implementation of a corrective regulation. Poor intermediaries or too many of them hinder reform.

But we need services to grow our businesses, and more importantly, we are willing and looking forward to working collectively: we call for a new generation of middlemen.

Hybrid services for an interwoven society:

The new middlemen have walked in our steps and want to be directly involved in our ventures. They are committed to profit-making *with* values. Interested in our business as a whole, they are knowledgeable about the parts they bring together.

The new middlemen have complementary skills. Trade jobs will benefit from being paired with research, design, and product development, or even with education. The salesperson who is also involved at other levels of the product chain will be more motivated. The profession will become more engaging for traders involved directly with product making or distribution, coaching, or brand strategies.

In our interwoven world we all become middlemen able to establish bridges between ideas, co-workers, or locations. Our creative sessions become a beautiful expression of middlemanship.

The dance of money and work:

Money too acts as a middleman.

It is a measurement of our success and power. Fiat money and gold have become a monopoly exchange standard that has phagocytized and outlawed other forms of currencies that can be traded directly and efficiently, such as time or services.

Money is a wonderful tool for exchange and it creates a flow of energy. It is a form of attention, and it amplifies every creation it touches, making it bigger, stronger, finer. But monetary despotism is the elephant in the room, an issue that we don't address at its core because changing our ways would have such radical implications. We would actually have to work and some of us are not used to it. This quote attributed to British Labour Party politician Baron Bruce Grocott sums it up well: "I have long been of the opinion that if work were such a splendid thing the rich would have kept more of it for themselves."

Money was invented as a promissory note, in return for which one had to render a good or service. We found ways around it so as to not give anything back. We forget to ask if and how our money-making operations serve others. Money is a conveniently abstract concept: We lost connection with the worth of things. When we make work a fulfilling experience we can rekindle with the notion of exchange. Money goes back to being a tool as opposed to a goal.

Talent as a currency:

There are more ways to trade.

We are starting to diversify our means of exchange, creating alternative currencies such as cryptocurrencies (bitcoins) or barter exchange platforms to provide labor. A case in point would be a system of redeemable points in return for hours of human labor. Barter is the original form of trade. It doesn't need to be the exclusive alternative to new ways of doing business. It can be adopted as an additional tool under our belt.

Creativity is a currency. It can be monetized and exchanged. The word *talent* means balance, weight, or a sum of money in classical Latin. It also refers to a special natural ability, an aptitude or a gift. Therefore, our project uses a currency called *talent*.

Inventiveness deserves a pedestal:

Folks in emerging countries show many creative resources. Necessity is the mother of invention. Remarkable agricultural solutions are seen in places where people have no choice but to come up with low-cost remedies for survival, using their ingenuity and everyday tools. Often those solutions are the most sustainable ones, because they harness the natural power of physics. Sometimes there is nothing like a good old latch to do the lock job; enough remote controls already, and nothing to worry about in case of power failure. The most basic solution can be the most efficient one. We are technological beings, and progress is amply advertised in the media. Yet we are also native to this planet; indigenous is who we forget we are.

The various applications of our project aim at introducing to the public creative individuals with common sense and practical craftsmanship, and encourage thereby the propagation of affordable solutions for those who don't necessarily have access to funding or modern amenities. It can also encourage us to invent our own simple solutions and share them with the world.

The advantage of making this project a journal is that it shows work in progress; when we are stuck in the development of a concept, we can call for help in the project's community to help develop the idea.

Entrepreneurship is contagious:

I once attended a lecture given by former U.S. Secretary of State Madeleine Albright to executive women in North America. In an atmosphere of debonair camaraderie and female solidarity, she delivered a speech encouraging the audience "to leave the ladder up after climbing to a position of power, for others to follow." Those who find ways to trade their creativity and make a profession out of it have the tremendous power to change society. Not only do they fulfill their own ambition but they also create jobs and become role models for others to become entrepreneurs.

Independent people grow an entrepreneurial spirit:

Automation, microtechnology, and all sorts of modern rental services that render our home and business chores easier make us increasingly independent. Our self-confidence is growing.

We are becoming empowered to step out and tell the world what we think of it. A movement like Occupy Wall Street has shown that an individual's voice counts and that inequality and greed can be denounced virally all over the globe. The Arab Spring waves of 2012 onward caused the downfall of entire governments. We no longer exhibit the same blind faith in our institutions, in our leaders, in the economy, and the corporate world.

In the United States there are already some 42 million freelancers,[120] some of whom are ready to take business to the next level and put employees on a payroll.

We are one step away from becoming entrepreneurs. We are just shy of a few beliefs.

The complications of becoming an entrepreneur:

We have not all been taught how to write sophisticated business plans. Yet some people have amazing ideas that will never see the light because the process is daunting.

Some manuals for the successful entrepreneur recommend incorporating a business where the sales taxes are the lowest, outsourcing to low-cost production havens, or setting up franchises with bank accounts offshore to avoid paying taxes. The logic behind these recommendations is understandable. Yet one has to be part of the old boys club to know all these tricks. It is intimidating to set up a business in a place where we don't live, or to seal deals with people whom we have never met. How do we finance the trips to meet with outsourced parties, pay translators to help us to communicate with foreigners, and hire supervisors who know the local culture to run operations?

These classic tips have made many entrepreneurs wealthy. But they present handicaps for the novice. There are so many intricacies in the fundraising market, so many pages to read in legal documents, so many business tools available on the market, that we need interpreters for the interpreters. We have turned to sly brokers, lawyers, bankers making a fortune mediating complexity. It looks like it is in our short-term interest to maintain and fuel more complications, to the point of absurdity. Complexity is beautiful, an impressive creation by savvy earthlings. But it shouldn't be the norm; we need simple cues to start a business.

There are many budding talents with a leader fiber who just need a template in the beginning to hold their creative spark and streamline their ideas. It is time to demystify the manual of entrepreneur and make the concept more accessible.

Local and scaled:

We can easily be tricked into growing a business that is larger than life when we are beginners. What if we're not interested in building quick cash, a large customer base, and selling our start-up to a large group after a few years or going public? What is the recipe for those who want to start small and stay local, with people they can create a bond with, and maintain the business just out of love for their trade?

Many regions in the world are demanding partition from the country they are affiliated with for economic reasons. The European Union is on the line, threatened by separatists. A form of economic protectionism flourishes among those with resources; isolationism is a discredited fantasy in our interconnected world, as discussed in chapter 7. Yet individuals who want to take governing matters into their own hands will find it easier to do so in smaller organizations. There, they can apply and nurture their entrepreneurial spirit.

Local businesses and businesses of measured capacity reinforce the middle class as the engine of a healthy economy, building household consumption power.

A marketplace for entrepreneurs:

With a simple frame of values and a strong sense of purpose, an individual can organize and strengthen an upcoming business model.

Undiscovered creativity is waiting to be deployed. On one side, some brilliant ideas need only a little push to be executed; on the other side, some folks ready to start a business would love to find out about them and participate in their manifestation. Wannabe inventors can meet wannabe venture capitalists directly and informally; they can have a go at their passions in a peer-to-peer mode. There is much creativity adrift in the meanderings of bureaucracy waiting to be expressed, provided folks with complementary skills find each other, across geo-cultural or socio-economic borders.

The project can encourage such a marketplace as a network for our creative endeavors.

This project aims at encouraging entrepreneurs of all backgrounds to set up a practice, interact with like-minded individuals, and barter skills.

This description of my values is a first personal step toward becoming my own entrepreneur. I take responsibility for my plan to form a company with a team that is inspired and engaged to build tools to define and promote our creative identity that are of use to the global community.

We want a marketplace for our own Hall of EXCHANGE.

This is an ENTERPRISE.

The tenth set of values is a tool to represent and market/trade/barter one's archetypal skills.

It marks one's tangible step towards becoming an entrepreneur in the marketplace.

Mercantile, entrepreneurial, and ambitious, the psychological archetype matching this part of our personality is THE MERCHANT.

11
UNDERSTAND

Tuning in to the
Collective Mind

Innovation, Instantaneity,
Inspiration, Intuition,
Public Spirit

At this eleventh hour of our wheel circle, our energy becomes multi-faceted. Quick-tempered like Uranus, or Ouranos, the ancient Greek god of heavens and ruler of Aquarius the eleventh zodiac entity, we become instant travelers of the psyche. We expand our identity, as we no longer fit in the confines of a single archetype, for this restricts our playfield.

A new polyvalent identity:

Uranus was discovered in 1781 during the Romantic period and was attributed qualities of inventiveness, freedom of expression, and humanism. In this energy, we are concerned with universal matters and the fortune of all. We are a part of the multitude. The boundaries of our identity start to dissolve.

As we zoom into the study of the minuscule, quantum mechanics tells us that the identity of a particle becomes versatile: Is it matter or is it light? "The wave-particle duality is a key principle in quantum theory, based on the observation that both matter at the subatomic level and light display properties of both wave and particle, that neither can be classified as simply a wave or a particle."[121]

Physicists Leopold Infeld and Albert Einstein wrote in *The Evolution of Physics* (1938):

> But what is light really? Is it a wave or a shower of photons? There seems no likelihood for forming a consistent description of the phenomena of light by a choice of only one of the two languages. It seems as though we must use sometimes the one theory and sometimes the other, while at times we may use

either. We are faced with a new kind of difficulty. We have two contradictory pictures of reality; separately neither of them fully explains the phenomena of light, but together they do.[122]

We are composed of those tiny entities. Our larger body is similarly tailored in this versatility; we are made both of matter and energy becoming interchangeable in the infinitesimally small, as the theory of General Relativity states. Nature and supernature, stuff and spirit are not only our attributes, they are the two contradictory and complementary constituents of our reality, making us whole.

Kaleidoscopic & schizophrenic:

Our human personality is a complex mix of who we think we are, who we have been taught to be, who we hope to be, and who we can become. Each day, we are internally governed by an array of feelings and sensations that make us swiftly and frequently alter our behavior. Micro-mood swings affect the way we think, we work, how we treat people, eat, or dress. We allow ourselves to be, act as, or look like a distinct version of ourselves, doing yoga or house chores in the morning, working during the day, and socializing in a crowded bar at happy hour. Notoriously skilled at this schizophrenic attitude, we live all these roles at once and we compose ourselves in a dazzling rainbow of concomitant visages. We accept this standard of ambivalence and welcome our multiple personality (dis)order as an opportunity to experience more, live fully, and create accordingly.

We grant ourselves more freedom of experimentation with our kaleidoscopic personalities.

Flickering & madness:

When we open up, the load of external stimuli and perpetual change tends to unsettle us. The mind is accustomed to finding stability in sameness and routine. We have been trained to understand earthly reality more easily when it is set and steady. Density is a state of being in slow motion. When our ordinary fans out into many possible ordinaries, we lose our footing, we have trouble telling realities apart. We drift away like a balloon in this vertiginous experience. Society calls us mad, sedates us, and locks us up.

The borders of our perception are porous:

Today, we need to learn to navigate a physical reality where boundaries are becoming more and more porous. Many tribal societies don't ostracize members disconnected from worldly matters as we still do in our mental wards. Instead, they call them wanderers of the spirit world; they keep them close and integrated into the social fabric. Sigmund Freud wrote a chapter called "Resemblances Between the Psychic Lives of Savages and Neurotics" in his work *Totem and Taboo*.[123] We have now crossed the fine line between savage and neurotic and made these attributes our own.

We call back those on the autism spectrum, as we recognize that they mirror our own shifts in the comprehension of our surroundings. We invite them into our work team, as we are curious about the way they perceive the environment; we recognize their vision as creative instead of unsuitable. We start to open up to the tangibility of parallel realities and even the possibility of alien planes of existence.

We are modern-day shamans:

Shamans are trained to hop from one state of consciousness to another. They have the ability to shape-shift, become comfortable within the elemental, floral, animal, or mineral worlds and merge with the realms of spirit. Through alteration of energetic vibration levels, they reach a mutable state of being, flitting between various aspects of their spirit and the global soul.

We achieve the ability to dissolve the stone walls erected between the various parts of our identity into fogs of mist, reconciling the two halves of our brain. Hazrat Inayat Khan says: "The soul in its manifestation on the earth is not at all disconnected from the higher spheres, although it is generally only conscious of one level. Only a veil separates us. The seer's own soul becomes a torch in his hand. It is his own light that illuminates his path. It is just like directing a searchlight into dark corners which one could not see before."[124]

The value system we are discussing here acts like a regulating valve for our creativity. From the center of our wheel, we layer the twelve different values inherent to our identity or our projects.

Increasing awareness:

As we dimension-hop from value to value, we gain self-confidence in our ability to shift what Carlos Castaneda refers to as the assemblage point of our perception, and perceive our internal world and the world around us with heightened awareness:[125]

> [...] 3. Human beings are also composed of an incalculable number of the same threadlike energy fields [...] a ball of light the size of the person's body with the arms extended laterally, like a giant luminous egg. 4. Only a very small group of the energy fields inside this luminous ball are lit up by a point of intense brilliance located on the ball's surface. [...] [t]hat point is named "the point where perception is assembled" or simply "the assemblage point.[...]"

We need "Seeing," or heightened awareness, to adjust to the craze of modern times, because it is the skill that allows us to slow the pace of a moment and stretch it to give us time to assess a situation and jump in for proper action. Heightened awareness dilutes density. It is our key to participating in the new fast game of life.

Radiant children:

New York artist Jean-Michel Basquiat was an outlet for tremendous creative forces.[126] Words and visuals rushed and trampled each other at the door of his awareness. He used several mediums to get the load of information out. With raw graffiti, drawing, paint, collage, or music he told us what we asked to hear about the SAMO or same-ol'[127] game of exploitation, consumption, and racism, a term that became his graffiti signature. He quickly made his way to public recognition. Like ultra-perceptive genius child-poets, actors, or musicians burned by fame at a very young age, he volunteered to anchor wisdom from higher dimensions and make society progress.

Nervous & excitable:

Information is feverish; profuse and diffuse, it pervades human perception. We jitter in multidirectional beams of synchronous data. With technology and global knowledge, the movies of our lives race to unfold; time flies by, days seem to be much shorter than the licit twenty-four hours. We must be vigilant in our choices for three reasons: a quickening of perception is taking place, we are increasingly skilled at creating, and what we give out spreads like a pandemic. Nervousness can be treacherous, but excitability is an opportunity. We snap at will; we zap our mental experience to rearrange our life narratives in no time.

Learning from technology to get instant feedback with the soul:

Modern communication is instantaneous and magical. The internet has become an intrinsic part of our mind, just as our technological devices have become extensions of our limbs.

It is now second nature for us to ask a question and receive an immediate response. We apply this skill to interact directly with our inner spiritual compass.

Recalibrating our perception:

We can be "online with ourselves" and tap into our inner source of wisdom. Stepping aside from the constrictions of physicality for a moment, we hear the faint voice of inner guidance and we start inquiring. We are developing the ability to connect our higher self to our conscious mind faster and in a smoother way. We recalibrate ourselves to switch back and forth from earthly living to a higher state. We merge with our spiritual essence. We no longer need to die in order to jump from the physical plane to the soul plane. We sway casually between dimensions without casualty.

Opening up to another's reality:

Time becomes space. We have the gift of ubiquity in this multiverse fashioned by us. A multidimensional canvas of facets in motion reveals a new playing field. We become the conductor of a symphonic movement of internal and global voices. Just as the internet is blurring the borders between countries or layers of society, we make the frontiers between individuals permeable. We start becoming aware of each other's intentions. We tap into the collective mind and retrieve information that affects the individual and the global, in the form of inspirational and intuitive hunches.

Inspiration is the engine to creativity:

Our thoughts are propagated through millions of impulses that circulate non-stop within our realm of perception. The brain holds close to 86 billion neurons, each with ten thousand connections. That amounts to quite an intricate mesh of activity.

Signals come through to our mind's awareness when we need them. Inspiration is available to help us focus on selected data at a particular moment, making us functional on this earthly plane, as well as creative. It is the whisper that slips through the walls of awareness and pollinates the creative intent of a fertile individual or group. Inspiration is a muse and a blessing: It is to creativity what sex is to impregnation, bringing that state of openness and bliss that allows us to create.

Intuition is awareness:

Like inspiration, the intuitive faculty is wrapped in mystery. Its seat is believed to be located in the pineal gland of the brain; philosopher and mathematician René Descartes viewed the pineal gland as "a little gland in the brain in which the soul exercises its function in a more particular way than in the other parts,"[128] or the principal seat of the soul. The first writings known about it are from a third century B.C. Greek physician called Herophilus; Hinduism affiliates it with the crown chakra and the Kabbalah with the Sephirot of Kether, both regarded as centers for spiritual development through which consciousness moves.[129]

Intuition has been deemed our sixth sense. It could be described as an overarching sense distributing data to each one of our five senses. It is a conduit between our mundane mind and the wise part of the self that is connected to the global brain.

Intuition as an inner conversation:

The process of anamnesis describes the recollection of knowledge from past incarnations. It implies that one knows the truth in its optimal form of wisdom through the soul, as Socrates states in Plato's *Phaedo:*[130] "But when it investigates by itself, it passes into the realm of the pure and everlasting and immortal and changeless, and being of a kindred nature, when it is once independent and free from interference, consorts with it always and strays no longer, but remains, in that realm of the absolute, constant and invariable, through contact with beings of a similar nature. And this condition of the soul we call wisdom."

Everyone has the ability to tap into an inner source of wisdom. The process of thought itself is an internal conversation. From Plato's *Dialogues* to Neal Donald's Walsh *Conversations with God*, these internal Q/As are accepted as a mode of thinking and have become a writing genre. Dialogues, conversations, confessions, meditations, all turn into international bestsellers when they reach the higher levels of brilliance where clarity triggers epiphanies, when they touch the soul of the masses, when they encourage readers to step up to their own bridge to wisdom.

Intuition acts as a messenger from the soul to the mind:

Intuitive impulses whisper messages to our perception in the form of impressions, images, words, thoughts, smells, or tastes. Information useful to us is delivered to our awareness through subtle hints that can be as anodyne as fragments of a conversation we overhear in a café, flashing pictures on a passing screen, or the scent of a plant nearby. These signals show up unannounced from uncommon sources while our attention scurries to control our environment. Once we acknowledge these signals, we discover that the data offered to us carries valuable suggestions and answers to critical and personal questions.

Trusting our intuition:

Intuition is a trustworthy detector. First, it is there for us, as long as we can think. Second, it is accurate. How many times do we hear ourselves say "I knew it." We have a gut feeling, and it is generally always the first impression that proves true.

I find that intuitive responses have a quality different from that of the mind's structured intellect. They have a crisp, neutral, even-toned,

155

and soft-spoken quality, and they pop up in my mind before I even finish formulating a mental question.

We don't always like the answers we receive through our intuitive processing system. Denial is probably a key reason why we have discarded this precious ability; we shot the messenger. Yet when we overcome fear, downplay reason, and eliminate judgment, when we disengage from our egotistic motives, we become impartial and we surrender to our intuition's signals.

Many artists find their way to express talent intuitively:

In a left-brain society, we have made a habit of discarding the value of intuition as unreliable and esoteric. I remember watching a video of Michael Jackson describing his song-writing process as spiritual, stating that he composed his songs, did the scoring, the lyrics, and the melody, but still, it was "the work of God."

Developing our intuition to express creativity:

Significantly, the process of channeling information from a higher source of knowledge is compared to birthing in the term *maieutics*. Maieutics are inspired by Plato's Socratic mode of inquiry and the pedagogical method of spiritual "midwifing" of anamnestic recollections into clear consciousness, where all knowledge is *already out there waiting to be given expression*. Once we are able to trust our intuition, we seize the opportunity to deliver value-able data to our perception and find inner guidance. Intuition is an engine for creation.

I have no doubt whatsoever that every thought written here has been said before, several times. Yet each time, it is expressed in a new collection according to the context du jour and the collective demand. I hope that the present compilation can add a fresh perspective to our contemporary needs.

Intuition is custom-tailored:

I believe that whatever information comes my way is a *personal gift to me.* It might not make any sense to someone else, and is only applicable to my life at a given moment. And if it doesn't ring relevant at this minute, it will in time. We absorb much information throughout the day unconsciously and store it in the back of our brain, miraculously digging it out later when the need arises. This storing occurs constantly, even if we are not aware of it.

A well-oiled intuition mechanism is our best news channel because it filters and distributes information that is customized wisely to our own needs. We have no obligation to watch all news shows and read all the newspapers, blogs, and magazines we can put our hands on to feel that we know enough. The time saved on seeking useless data can be applied to utilizing useful data. We can rely on what seeks our attention, be it sound or thought, wind or tide, living being or inanimate thing. These elements demand access to us, and they carry important messages.

A decryption system:

We all listen to inner guidance and translate it in our own way. Some people perceive intuitive signals as a "download," a nonlinear packet of information that they have the brain software to detangle and decrypt. Kryon, an entity channeled by a medium consulted at several occasions at United Nations assemblies,[131] describes this "download" phenomenon best with the analogy of an old typewriter with a stuck carriage: as one types, characters pile up on top of each other in one single smudge that is illegible to the common eye.[132] Yet one with the proper decoding system can isolate the characters and eventually lay them next to each other in the linear order that permits deciphering.

Intuition gym:

The muscle of intuition can be trained. As we sample intuitive messages, we establish a psychic medium between our individual awareness and collective records. After extensive meditation training, one can experience moments of permeability between inner and outer reality, and establish ties between facts, events, or conversations seemingly unrelated around us. When we develop our intuition, we tune into the collective consciousness, we learn to listen. Our responses to life become accurate. Over time, we build trust in our ability to discern.

Intuition is a global channel:

Intuition is a signalization system, pushing impulses to our attention and repeating them until they are finally acknowledged. Signals concentrate at a global level, propagate virally through cyber or telepathic communication, and crystallize into a piece of information that can be perceived clearly by many. All signals come from and evolve in the global pool of data, where linear time doesn't exist. Chicken or egg question—it is impossible to tell which individual started it.

I give credit to the collectivity for this idea of creating a system of "relating" based on ancient values. In that sense, this material is not mine only, even if I might experience it as such. An intuitive part of me captures a universal desire and channels it. I volunteer to bring it to the world, if the world wants it. I make myself the vehicle of something that is already hovering in the realm of probabilities. The idea happens to match my frequency; it asks to be manifested using my particular skills and enthusiasm. All I need to do is claim responsibility for it.

It will become harder to predict the timing of outcomes as we collectively become aware of our own power to read the world and influence the fate of civilization.

Intuition, art and public benefit:

Artists are oracles with high-performance antennae finely tuned to catch signals from the intuitosphere before they manifest, and lay them on the altar of global awareness. We are the canaries in the coal mine that expose collective desires and distortions.

Art is a necessity of humanitarian importance. Art is a missing link between the desire of one and the will of all.

Following one's intuition is a recipe for success:

Every one of us is a potential artist who has the capacity to capture signals, especially with topics that we are passionate about. What excites us, what we care about, is what we download data about most effortlessly from the collective database. When we follow our intuition wholeheartedly, we become experts at these subjects dear to us, to the point where we can make them our main life activity or profession. Success guaranteed.

Intuitive marketing:

This project inspires the user to inform, and get informed by, the overall aggregation of creative treasures. It is an open door to the collectivity, giving us a chance to satisfy our curiosity toward another's magic.

It is a tool to listen to and sort out signals pertaining to our favorite subjects: We can become masters of what captivates us the most. Once we apply this skill to our professional enterprises, we can develop a form of intuitive marketing that will help us to stay connected at all times with the demands of the universal mind.

We need an exchange platform in our Hall of TRAVEL.

This is a HUB.

The eleventh set of values calls for a broadcasting tool to share storybooks across the globe. Gaining access to other people's stories will help us to strengthen our intuition as our hunches are confirmed.

This newsroom asks for a technical tool to record multiple actions/stories on the site and make them public.

Technological renderings such as digital visualization are used to make the platform appealing and data understandable at a glance.

It uses a form of GPS showing threads of interaction over the planet.

Futuristic, global, and as fast as light, the psychological archetype matching this part of our personality is THE TRAVELER.

12

RECONCILE

Integrating Our Creative Fragments

Completion, Centering, Unity, Heart

From fragmentation to integration:

This book starts with a personal story, and it ends with the value of completion. From cool to wise, from self to soul, from one to many, from elements to archetypes, from fear to trust, from doubt to knowledge, from abstraction to manifestation, from spirit to business, from mind to heart, from 1 to 12, the journey is long.

Our project has added balance with the number 7, transmutation power with the number 8, stories to tell with the number 9, an entrepreneurial sprit with the number ten, and intuitive skills with the number eleven. Now we are ready to sum it all up.

Like the final limb of the discipline of yoga seeking *samadhi*, or self-collectedness, this wheel is an integrative tool to reunite the disparate elements of our personalities and of our projects.

It acts as a manual of instruction to establish continuity between our internal gaps and unite our teams.

Togetherness is the strongest fundamental force:

Out of the four fundamental forces that science has identified so far—the electromagnetic force, the gravitational force, the strong force, and the weak force—the most powerful one is the residual strong force, which maintains the nuclei of an atom together. Its power is mostly attractive. It takes this formidable bonding force for the geometry of nucleons to set and to hold, allowing the manifestation of matter to last. All things exhibited in our physical reality are the result of bonding, and one could say, a pure show of atomic love. Whether constructive or destructive, whether we perceive it as beautiful or dreadful, every co-creation is to be respected as a tour de force of togetherness.

Reuniting with spirit:

There is great metaphorical puissance in the concept of animism. Anima is the Latin word for *soul*; animism is the belief that a spiritual force animates every object, plant, or natural phenomenon. For adepts of animism, spirit dwells within matter and lives on after decomposition. It brings to awareness the presence of dead ancestors and establishes spiritual perpetuation throughout the lineage of the earth's species.

Lineage of biology:

Our biology is the manifestation of what we are in physical reality. Within the base structure of each cell are contained the seeds for its own evolution. All things go through the processes of growing, burgeoning, blossoming, withering, dying, dismantling, and recomposing into new form.

Human biology is a link to our ancestry and to the universe:

Scientifically, every molecule composing our bodies is the product of a long series of genetic merging and division of our forbears' cells. Through our metabolism, with vital functions such as breathing and digestion, we absorb nutrients, minerals, and water from our environment. Every atom in our body is a product of planetary recycling. The quantity of water available on the planet is constant[133] and reprocessed through the hydrologic workings of evaporation, condensation, precipitation, and transpiration. It is the same water molecules that have traveled through plants, minerals, and creatures since life started on earth. A well-known (and disputed) 1999 experiment on water using high-speed photography showed how music, words written on paper, or emotional stimuli affect the shapes of freezing crystals of water. Masaru Emoto's book, *The Hidden Messages in Water,*[134] describes how water exposed to heavy metal music or the word *fool* resulted in fragmented crystals, while that exposed to Beethoven's or Mozart's symphonies or the words *thank you* appeared symmetrical. This experiment raises the question of whether water is connected with individual and collective consciousness. What if our water molecules bear memory?

Cells united by their memory?

We know little about cell intelligence; it is so small. Maybe science will come to re-assess the definition of life itself once it finds a way to magnify the minuscule even more. Maybe some day the tribulations of particles will be made visible to the human eye. Maybe this memory is alive within our water-filled human structure and impacts our everyday behavior. Like the Pando quaking aspen grove in Utah,[135] all growing from the same root system in a rhizome formation to create a forest that is one massive clone, we may be part of a giant organism of collective memory held together by the vibration of our cells. If this is the case, we are walking around with a load of graces and burdens billions of times bigger than the genome of our direct ancestry. We discussed earlier our cerebral ability to access the global memory of the world. I like to think that we have *cellular* access to the vast hall of records of global information, conferring to biological beings an innate cognition of humanity and giving us the opportunity to use it wisely.

Creation is re-membering:

We are ready to embark on a journey of remembering who we are, like the Egyptian god Osiris, dismembered into fourteen pieces by his brother Seth and re-membered by his sister Isis, who conceived their child Horus posthumously with his recollected body. The legend tells the story of a lost lover pieced together by enduring love, insuring continued creation, as Horus is a multilayered deity and perhaps the most famous of all Egyptian gods.

This myth is an analogy for re-membrance. It can be transcribed as a reintegration of the fragmented human perception: We forget who we are and we have a hard time recalling the larger view that we are

165

part of. Without completion we are not able to conceive, or by extension, to create.

We use drugs to unblock the barriers elevated by reason or trauma, to enable the reconnection of the mind to the big picture of creation. But when the drug effect subsides, we slump back to the sarcophagus of our locked perception, right where we left off.

Re-membering our ideal:

A re-membering exercise is vital to experiencing completion.

We take the multiple faces of our identity by the hand and escort them back to the core. A brand is patched together to reconstitute its lost image. Team workers regroup the strongest characteristics necessary for the success of a business project. Our job is to recollect all the virtual bits of a dream and reconstruct it as best we can.

We recall that desired version of ourselves, of a brand, of a project that exists on a potential timeline; all we need to do is let its beauty come through and manifest.

As I write this material, I spiral on a voyage to remember my values. I piece the fragments of my research with deductions from my life experiences. Through these twelve chapters I bring homogeneity to the various possible applications of this project. I retrace my steps to the concept that is already completed on a larger cohesive plane of existence. I ask to be shown what it looks like.

The *abundance* of the number 12:

We discussed how the number 12 offers a sound structure for creative exploration in chapter 6. Let's look at the big picture.

In arithmetic number theory, 12 is the first *abundant* number. It is the "first number for which the sum of its proper divisors is greater than the number itself. Its proper divisors are 1, 2, 3, 4, and 6 for a total of 16. The amount by which the sum exceeds the number, 4 in this case, is called the abundance."[136]

In a way, 12 surpasses itself. It certainly supersedes my expectations as I journal this material.

Many teachings use the number 12 as a reference and a guideline. It offers a casing to many of our measurements.

Some are cultural measurements, such as hours in a day and the number of months of the Julian calendar. Inches, pounds, angles, and degrees have been organized duodecimally. Octaves of our Western common musical grid have twelve musical semitones. Chinese medicine describes twelve principal meridians as the vehicles of our energetic *qi*. Some are biological measurements, such as the quantity of cranial nerves spreading from our brain to our spinal cord. Some are mythical measurements like the collection of epic poems that make up *The Twelve Labors of Hercules,* the twelve disciples of Christ, the Book of Revelations' Twelve Tribes of Israel or the Chinese and Western astrology zodiac systems referred to here.

In numerical base 9, twelve is reduced to three (1+2=3) and holds within its frame the magic inherent to this symbol of creation and physical manifestation, as seen in our third chapter.

In Western astrology, the twelfth and last constellation is that of Pisces and is inspired by the myth of Neptune/Poseidon, ruler of the water world of which life originates. Piscean energy is one of faith toward the complementarity of man in his spiritual and physical forms. It believes in infinity.

Holon geometry, a link between infinity and individuality:

Once all fragments of a project, an event, a person, or a brand are reconciled, the whole becomes more than the sum of its parts. The geometric three-dimensional figure called a Klein bottle presents an infinite loop composed of two Möbius strips connected back to back. In a funnel rolled into itself, a bit like a twisted donut, this form presents a case of what philosophy calls a holon: A system, an organism, or a phenomenon that is simultaneously a whole and a part. Anglo-Hungarian journalist Arthur Koestler introduced the term *holon* in the 1960s in reference to a hierarchical system in society functioning "as self-contained wholes," embracing the "dichotomy of wholeness and apartness, of autonomy and dependence."[137] Some

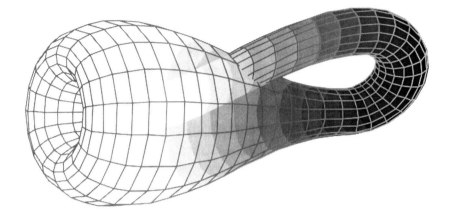

cosmology theorists liken the universe to a membrane shaped in a holon[138] structure, with interpenetrating dimensions that never collide yet bleed onto each other like tinctures, allowing for imbuement and absorption.

This figure potentially depicts the missing link that we have been looking for between the divine and the individual. We permute from object to subject. I like to think that our consciousness functions like a holon and that we are unified and merged with the universe, while being a part of it at the same time. From this perspective, we are nudged into making the sensible choices that benefit all involved.

I am interested in creating an online structure that allows a looping flow between each archetype and the twelve values, between the individual and the crowd.

Interconnectedness of being becomes possible, which is ultimately what everybody wants to believe.

Ego consciousness is drifting away:

The human heart is elated at the concept of interconnectedness. We long to belong. When we stand in our truth, we believe that the universe will allow nothing short of the ideal we seek. Belonging and love for our next of kin provides a euphoria much more potent than ego-driven satisfaction, an exhilaration demonstrated in large solidarity social movements. When we distrust our own power of love we level on the lower vibration of competition or conquest, and we expel ourselves from the global mega party. Egotistic consciousness cuts itself loose, drifts out without purpose, a lonely consciousness wandering without an anchor and trying to hold on in a last élan of stubbornness and desperate show of fanaticism.

Aligning the mind to a higher purpose:

Ego is necessary for our individuation process, to help the mind mark healthy boundaries of identity between an individual and its surroundings, boundaries without which we could not provide for the basics needs of our material existence.

Yet on a spiritual level we are all reflections of the same unified mind creating itself endlessly. Once the mind realizes this unity, it lets the heart lead.

The mind doesn't know, because its purpose is to question. The heart knows, because its purpose is to connect.

The disheartening of our society:

We have been hurt when opening our hearts to others. We can be mindful but evidently not enough in this unequal community, in which a small fraction of us owns the largest portion of the world's resources. The major issue of our civilization, as hippie as it sounds, is a heart issue.

In *Le Petit Prince* (1943) by French philosopher and poet Antoine de Saint-Exupery, the fox says: *"Voici mon secret. Il est très simple: on ne voit bien qu'avec le coeur. L'essentiel est invisible pour les yeux."* Here is my secret. It is very simple: one sees well only with the heart. The essential is invisible to the eyes.[139]

Broken communication:

The difficulty I encounter while writing this material reflects the challenge to verbalize the connection between the spiritual and the physical. Business is about what works and what doesn't; it asks concise questions and wants yes or no answers. Spirit is wide open, it speaks in endless nuances.

The fundamental differences between the language of the soul and the language of physical reality impair communication. For instance, killing is obviously a despicable act in our physical reality; declaring otherwise will make most people leave the room. However, in an etheric language, killing is the very action without which one couldn't understand the consequences of murder; in that sense it is a useful lesson.

Another basic example is that of geocentrism. We learned with Copernicus that our planet orbits the sun, and not the other way around. But from where I stand today, undoubtedly the sun revolves around me.

A third example shows that darkness, which we all know affects the world in despicable aspects, in fact doesn't exist: St. Augustine, the scholar crucial to the foundation of western Christianity and philosophy to this day and an inspirer to St. Thomas Aquinas' reflections, attributes the syndrome of human imbalance to darkness, which he simply states as an absence of light:

> And God said, "Let there be light."(Gen 1:3). He said this because there is no light, there is darkness, not because darkness is something; rather the very absence of light is called darkness.[...] Thus [the Manichees] suppose that darkness is something, and they do not understand that darkness is only perceived when we do not see, as silence is perceived when we do not hear. But as silence is nothing, darkness is nothing.[140]

Everybody is right:

Truth is to be accepted wherever it is found, as Thomas Aquinas proposes.[141] Whether they agree or contradict each other, schools of thought all have a point, adding to their forefathers' views, whether by development or by rebuttal, and laying bricks for future finds. Controversy might be a marketing tool, but it is necessary in its own time as it wakes us up and makes us think. I respect thinkers of all times whose views might today appear as outdated yet were precursors of their time, busting open the doors of public understanding and allowing future peers to refine knowledge according to the new standards of modernity.

Some views offer immediate resolutions and some others work on the long run. Some issues are small and some others affect a larger number of people.

The art of love:

Everybody is right over time and/or over scope, but imagine all these great thinkers debating under one roof; some congressional cacophony it would produce, ending in gridlock. Nothing would get done.

Today we know our own mind games like the backs of our hands; we have played them over and over and they feel like a tight glove. Pain is louder than ease and we realize that we have let the screaming of suffering talk over the quiet voice of wellness. The mind has the power to create from thought, but it is only when we put this thought in our heart that the intention is warmed up, the resonance magnified and radiated from an individual's center to ripple out and benefit ever- larger circles of recipients.

We are entering a period where mankind acknowledges that its happiness and that of the collectivity are interdependent. When one part is at war, the whole is mobilized for a solution. When one bit is ailing, the whole is on healing alert, just as the whole body mobilizes to heal the cut finger.

Sun Tzu's sixth-century B.C. treatise *The Art of War* is a literary work on military tactics popular among 1990s businessmen desirous to take action for corporate success. Today, The Art of War becomes The Art of Love, the great war worth fighting. We shell small minds with compassion to relearn the paths of the heart.

As American psychologist Jacquelyn Small states: "We must learn a way to offer the world a way of approach that honors the ego's desire to be holy and the soul's true delight to be all-too-human."[142]

Who is talking now, mind or heart? Training for peace of mind:

Everybody is doing the best they can. We mean well, we have ethics. But how durable are our solutions? Who do our values pledge allegiance to? Our persona, our tribe or the world? How large is our scope? How big is our heart? How many people, things, facts, and possibilities can it contain and serve? Size matters. We are ready for bigger and better. We have outrun our chances of fixing environmental, economic, and social issues with quick solutions; we don't have a choice anymore, We must learn to assess whether we speak from soul or from ego, and state it.

We nest our mind within our heart; relieved from its obligations as master, the mind is asked to serve. It must be overworked by all this micromanagement; with all the turmoil we go through our egos are on the brink of a burnout. Time to enjoy a mind break.

Yet we have homework to do: Mind or heart talking? This simple question can be asked before each one of our affirmations. This exercise will help us shift our operation headquarters to the heart center. It will also produce emotional relief to the honest and loving part of our psyche; all told, thinking from the heart will give us peace of mind.

Creativity is a heart-driven solution:

We can commit to self-observation. Sometimes the imperatives of survival and emotional blocks make it hard for us to get out of our own way. Some folks don't have the luxury to do their karmic, psychic, and emotional laundry, and some folks just don't enjoy introspection. For some of us, the best way to balance body and soul is to stay focused on basic activities; tasks such as cooking, cleaning, or gardening ground us. They make us feel safe and connected to our original nature. The outdoors brings wisdom and common sense to our hearts. *In puris naturalibus,* in a state of nature. Everyone has his or her own technique, and there is no wrong way.

Our heartbeat is fully committed:

The human heart is a muscular pump that has the particularity to follow the all-or-none law: it has a strength independent of the strength of the stimulus that caused it. It means that the heart muscle contracts to the full extent of its potential under a stimulus strong enough to be detected, unlike other muscle tissues that contract in proportion to a stimulus' strength. The heart is sure. No hesitation. Once motivated it always gives it all it's got.

In helping us to explore our values, the project helps us to ascertain our art so that we can give it all our might.

The heart metaphor:

The user is always connected to the center of the wheel. The platform facilitates pulsations back and forth from the heart of the wheel to the archetypes' energies on the periphery. Navigation radiates from the center outward, to contract back again.

Let us give it a chance and see if this system mirrors interaction from our own heart to our mind, with no other central authority than our soul, which is not only in direct connection with Source, but *is* Source.

Intimacy is the glue for integration:

This project offers a way to walk around the circle of twelve different realities, each of them offering a lamellar and complementary scope of the same generic entity. The ingredient mandatory to completion is intimacy. Intimacy is the glue that binds constituents. It is an eraser of differences. It is the ultimate value that permits integration of the whole, and the true essence of love in all its forms. The configuration of the platform allows for intimacy between the various facets of the self, of a project, of a brand, of an organization. The journaling activity permits continuous monitoring and binding of our creative activities.

Our wheels are mandalas of completion:

The symbol of the wheel reflects the desire for completion. C.G. Jung was particularly inspired by the concept of the Indian mandala, the center of which he saw as: "The energy of the central point [of a mandala] is manifested in the almost irresistible compulsion and urge to *become what one is*, just as every organism is driven to assume the form that is characteristic of its nature, no matter what the circumstances. This center is not felt or thought of as the ego but, if one may so express it, as the *self*."[143]

Completion, integration and integrity:

Love dissolves us into the formlessness of the collective soul. We *become* the global intent. Our creativity is the spark that animates our physical world. The health of a project is linked to the health of all its components. The success of a team or company is ultimately linked to that of each of its members. The twelve values of our system form an integrative piece where each value asks to be heard. Integration leads to personal and collective progress.

As we journal in the intimacy of our wheels, we integrate our known and unknown parts. We complete our mission in the highest vibration in line with our heart's desire. We reach integrity through integration. We watch ourselves unfold at our chosen pace in harmony with the creative community.

We find grace in the temple that is our Hall of CONTEMPLATION.

This is a PRACTICE.

The twelfth and final set of values is a rewarding system for all activity performed on the site.

Whole, centered and able to merge with the collective psyche the psychological archetype matching this part of our personality is THE SAGE.

13

LUCKY CHAPTER

I retrospectively consider the challenge the writing of this material has demanded of me. It has allowed me to be, if you'll permit the dreaded expression, born again into the idealist that I never ceased yet was conflicted to be.

I have read of words that describe my "condition" and felt equally happy when I found philosophical references backing optimism as when I found refutation of it. It made me ascertain my positions and convince the two halves of my brain to respect each other within the vaster conciliating love of my heart. I found the verb I needed to introduce this project to the world.

Leibniz's *Principle of Continuity* makes the point of those eager to bring spiritual values to everyday affairs. His thought in the Preface to the *New Essay that* "Nothing takes place suddenly, and it is one of my great and best confirmed maxims that *nature never makes leaps*"[144] is a translation of the Latin phrase *Natura non facit saltum*, attributed to Aristotle in relation to his research on causality. This powerful statement appeals to spiritualists and scientists alike. Those believing in the existence of a united consciousness refer to this principle of continuity, and Charles Darwin quotes this phrase in his *On the Origin of Species*. The theory of evolution of corporate codes—if there is such a thing—honors the relativity between human resources, work processes, and products. Those values that make us successful have filtered through from ancient times to modernity and from spirit to business.

On this earthly plane, we simply cannot burn the steps of our biological, psychological, and socioeconomic progressions; neither the body nor the mind will allow us to skip a grade in their evolution. Even the honor student, as fast as she may learn, will climb every step of apprenticeship in a continuous movement. Humanity chooses linearity as its MO in spacetime continuum. Every kind of motion goes through gradations of grays. This powerful realization constitutes evidence for interconnectedness in the physical world. We know the soul levitates in a unified world, because it is its nature; so do matter and facts in the physical world. As above, so below indeed. Three-dimensional reality is a simplified replica of the multidimensional matrix of our larger selves. Our goals are all attainable, provided we are willing to walk the entire succession of bridges. Continuity is the meaning behind the spiral symbol revered by civilization since prehistoric times. It is the legacy of mankind and its connection with the divine. By nature we cannot be any other way. We are unbroken.

The spiral of continuity gives a sense to the digital platform I was only imagining so far: It makes it a place where users can increase their creativity *gradually* and *collectively*.

We can achieve whatever we want. Creativity is infinite. The wheel is a place where we gather missing links to ascend to happier states of being. It's as easy as pie. Let us spiral divinely in honor of the DNA we are made of.

This project wears twelve names. It can be an act, a resource, an intervention, a family, a play, a structure, a movement, an experiment, a culture, an enterprise, a hub, and a practice.

I am grateful to the numbers and the archetypal energies that inspired this experiment.

I thank the participants in this co-creation, the readers for their reading, and the potential anonymous in other realms extending their kindred spirit onto these considerations.

Friends, we are knocking on heaven's door. Let us reflect to one another the divine attributes within.

Today we upgrade from earthling to angel. This material introduces the project *Angelings*, a tool for creative integration.

From numbers and sacred geometry, it made its way through words and values to our attention. As an earthly manifestation, our project is a living entity claiming its own sweet name to break the seriousness.

It doesn't know itself; it is up to us participants to encourage its becoming, including the multitude of interferences that will shape its fate.

I am delighted to watch it evolve and see how we steer the wheel.

We are coming full circle.

In love and gratitude,
Emmanuelle

ENDNOTES

1   Bamon, Leopoldo Garcia. "Correspondance; Le Noel En Espagne." *Le Monde Illustre* 12.15 (1871): 402. *Google Books*. Web. 14 Oct. 2014. Spanish & French idiomatic expression: an empty seat at the Christmas table left for the occasional vagabond: *"Entre la mère et l'aïeule, il y a aussi une place vide, une place que l'on appelle la place du pauvre ; rarement le souper finit sans qu'elle ne soit occupée par un malheureux qui n'a d'autre famille que celle que la Providence lui donne pour quelques heures"*. English Translation: Between the mother and the foremother, there is also an empty seat called the place of the poor: rarely does the supper end without this seat being occupied by a poor soul whose only family is that of fate given to him for a few hours.

2   Platon, and Paul Shorey. *The Republic.* London: William Heinemann, 1963. Print. Aristotle, and David Keyt. *Politics.* Oxford: Clarendon, 1999. Print.

3   Schopenhauer, Arthur. *The World as Will and Idea.* London: Everyman, 2004. 44–45. Print. After Leibniz's Dissertation De Principio Individui originally published in May 1663, Schopenhauer uses the term *principium individuationis* to describe one's awareness of existence within space and time.

4   The Editors of Encyclopædia Britannica. "Wujing (Chinese Texts)." *Encyclopedia Britannica Online.* Encyclopedia Britannica, n.d. Web. 14 Oct. 2014. "Wuji" or "Wu Chi": from standard Chinese "without ridgepole" meaning "ultimateless, boundless, infinite" in Warrior States Period Daoist classics, period 476–221 BC. The term came to mean "Primordial Universe" in Song Dynasty (960–1279 BC) Neo-Confucianist cosmology.

5   The Editors of Encyclopædia Britannica. "Tat Tvam Asi (Hinduism)." *Encyclopedia Britannica Online.* Encyclopedia Britannica, n.d. Web. 14 Oct. 2014.

6   Process described by the Oxford dictionary—as the action by which a person claims to be in contact with the spirits of the dead and can communicate between the dead and the living. I find it reductive to limit the process of channeling to communication with the dead. I personally was rather open to call out and establish contact with any form of energy or intelligence, including the possibly of my own, in various shapes. I therefore call it by the general term of intuitive channeling.

7   Echols, Signe E., Robert E. Mueller, and Sandra A. Thomson. *Spiritual Tarot: Seventy-eight Paths to Personal Development*. New York: Avon, 1996. 42–44. Print.

8   "The Revelation of St. John The Divine, 1:1" *Holy Bible: Authorized King James Version*. Grand Rapids, MI: Zondervan, 2009. 1747–1724. Print.

9   Plato, Edith Hamilton, and Huntington Cairns. "Phaedo 78c, 78d." Trans. Hugh Tredennick. *The Collected Dialogues of Plato, including the Letters*. Princeton, NJ: Princeton UP, 1961. 61–62. Print. Bollingen Ser. LXXI.

10 "Abraham Lincoln's Crucial Formative Years." *History Press Blog*. N.p., 12 Nov. 2012. Web. 14 Oct. 2014. <www.historypressblog.net/2012/11/27/abraham-lincolns-formative-years/>.

11 Covert, Bryce. "CEOs Earn Nearly 300 Times What Their Workers Make." *Think Progress RSS*. N.p., 12 June 2014. Web. 18 Nov. 2014.

12 Salford, Leif G., Arne E. Brun, Jacob L. Eberhardt, Lars Malmgren, and Bertil R. R. Persson. "Abstract." *National Center for Biotechnology Information*. U.S. National Library of Medicine, 22 Nov. 0005. Web. 14 Oct. 2014.

13 "EMF Pollution from Living Near Power Lines - Solved?" *EMF Pollution from Living Near Power Lines - Solved?* Dimensional Design Products, Inc., 2013. Web. 14 Oct. 2014.

14 Rosaler, Josh. "The Oxonian Review » An Interview with Brian Greene." *The Oxonian Review RSS*. The Oxonian Review, 4 Apr. 2011. Web. 14 Oct. 2014. Theoretical physicist Brian Greene states in an interview with Oxonian Review "If you're willing to view religion more in a Spinozan or even Einsteinian way—that there is an overarching order and harmony that the laws of physics represent and reveal, and that order and harmony, if you want, ascribe it to some deeper theological origin—then I don't think science has much to say about that. What science is pretty good at ruling out is the so-called "God of the gaps"—the traditional way of invoking God whenever there's something in science that we haven't figured out. [...]".

15 The word "Source" is used here to refer to the above-quoted concepts of The Absolute, Wuji, or Ultimate Reality. Capitalized here to differentiate from the concept of human source as related to our biological birth.

16 Wang, Kangli, Kai Jiang, Brice Chung, Takanari Ouchi, Paul J. Burke, Dane A. Boysen, David J. Bradwell, Hojong Kim, Ulrich Muecke, and Donald R. Sadoway. "Lithium–antimony–lead Liquid Metal Battery for Grid-level Energy Storage." *Nature.com*. N.p., 16 Oct. 2014. Web. 19 Nov. 2014. "The ability to store energy on the electric grid would greatly improve its efficiency and reliability while enabling the integration of intermittent

renewable energy technologies (such as wind and solar) into base load supply 1, 2, 3, 4. Batteries have long been considered strong candidate solutions owing to their small spatial footprint, mechanical simplicity and flexibility in siting. However, the barrier to widespread adoption of batteries is their high cost. Here we describe a lithium–antimony–lead liquid metal battery that potentially meets the performance specifications for stationary energy storage applications."

17   Diep, Francie. "An All-Liquid Battery For Storing Solar And Wind Energy."*Popular Science*. N.p., 2 Sept. 2014. Web. 19 Nov. 2014.

18   Keller, Michael. "Key To LED Lighting Revolution Wins Three Physics Nobel." *Txchnologist*. General Electric, 7 Oct. 2014. Web. 19 Nov. 2014.

19   King, Leonard William. *The Seven Tablets of Creation, or the Babylonian and Assyrian Legends concerning the Creation of the World and of Mankind, Edited by L. W. King,..* London: Luzac, 1902. Print; Reiner, Erica. "Part 2: Enuma Any Enlil." *Babylonian Planetary Omens*. Malibu: Undena Publ., 1981. N. pag. Tablets 50–51. Print. Pingree, David Edwin, and Reiner, Erica. "Enlil, Enûma Anu." "Part 1: The Venus Tablet of Ammisaduqa, Enuma Anu Enlil." *Babylonian Planetary Omens*. Malibu, Calif: Undena Publ., 1975. N. pag. Tablet 63. Print. Seven clay tablets written in Sumero-Akkadian cuneiform script between the 18th and 16th century BC, describing the creation of the universe. A tale inspired by the more ancient Sumer civilization (appr. 5,500–2000 BC).

20   Peters, F. E. *Greek Philosophical Terms; a Historical Lexicon*. New York: New York UP, 1967. 23–24. Print.

21   Plato, Edith Hamilton, and Huntington Cairns. "Timaeus Dialogue, 53c3–6, 54cd, 55abc." *The Collected Dialogues of Plato, including the Letters*. Princeton, NJ: Princeton UP, 1961. 1180–181. Print. Bollingen Ser. LXXI. Pythagoras (c. 570–495 BC) didn't leave written traces of his teachings. The notion of elements is attributed to the Pythagoreans (originated in 500 BC) and was transcribed in written form by Plato in 360 BC in the Timaeus Dialogue.

22   Dean, Bartholomew. *Urarina Society, Cosmology, and History in Peruvian Amazonia*. Gainesville: U of Florida, 2009. Print.

23   "The global voice of Wikipedia": even if Wikipedia is not quite accepted as a citation source among scholars, it represents a glorified example of a modern crowd-generated attempt at encyclopedic knowledge. Despite its state of pending impermanence and inconclusiveness, Wikipedia is a source that feels at home in this material devoted to continual co-creation and business inspiration. I use the bibliography references regularly.

24 Escher, M. C. *The Magic of M. C. Escher*. N.p.: Thames & Hudson, 2000. Print. Reprinted 2006.

25 Epictetus, and Robert F. Dobbin. "Book 1, Chapter 15, What Philosophy Professes." *Discourses and Selected Writings*. London: Penguin, 2008. 40. Print.

26 Aristotle. *"XVII METAPHYSICS I-IXNYPL"*. N.p.: Research Libraries 3 3433 07673217 5, n.d. 2+. Print. "The theory of a universal science, as sketched by Plato in The Republic, was unsatisfactory to Aristotle's analytical mind. He felt that there must be a regular system of sciences, each concerned with a different aspect of reality. At the same time it was only reasonable to suppose that there is a supreme science which is more ultimate, more exact, more truly wisdom than any of the others. The discussion of this science – Wisdom, Primary Philosophy or Theology [...] and of its scope forms the subject of the Metaphysics.". Inwagen, Peter Van. "Metaphysics." *Stanford University*. Stanford University, 10 Sept. 2007. Web. 14 Oct. 2014. "The word 'metaphysics' is derived from a collective title of the fourteen books by Aristotle that we currently think of as making up "Aristotle's Metaphysics." Aristotle himself did not know the word. [...] At least one hundred years after Aristotle's death, an editor of his works (in all probability, Andronicus of Rhodes) entitled those fourteen books "Ta meta ta phusika"—"the after the physicals" or "the ones after the physical ones"—, the "physical ones" being the books contained in what we now call Aristotle's Physics."

27 Monroe, Robert A. *Far Journeys*. Garden City, NY: Doubleday, 1985. Print.

28 "Definition of Space-time in English:." *Space-time: Definition of Space-time in Oxford Dictionary (American English) (US)*. N.p., n.d. Web. 14 Oct. 2014. <www.oxforddictionaries.com/us/definition/american_english/space-time?q=space+time>.

29 "Definition of Singularity in English:." *Singularity: Definition of Singularity in Oxford Dictionary (British & World English)*. N.p., n.d. Web. 14 Oct. 2014. <www.oxforddictionaries.com/definition/english/singularity>. "Spacetime singularity: Physics & Mathematics: a point at which a function takes an infinite value, especially in spacetime when matter is infinitely dense, as at the center of a black hole."

30 Knapp, Alex. "A Black Hole Brings New Stars To Life." *Forbes*. Forbes Magazine, n.d. Web. 14 Oct. 2014. <www.forbes.com/sites/alexknapp/2012/02/07/a-black-hole-brings-new-stars-to-life/>.

31 Knight, Gareth. "Volume 1, Part II, Chapter IX." *A Practical Guide to Qabalistic Symbolism*. Boston: Weiser, 2001. 103. Print.

32 Knight, Gareth. "Volume 1, Part I, Chapter III." *A Practical Guide to Qabalistic Symbolism*. Boston: Weiser, 2001. Fig. 1 (Sephirots). 24–25. Print.

33 Elk, Black, and John Gneisenau Neihardt. *Black Elk Speaks: Being the Life Story of a Holy Man of the Oglala Sioux*. Lincoln: U of Nebraska, 1988. 192. Print. " I will say something about the heyokas and the heyoka ceremony, which seems to be very foolish, but is not so. Only those who have had visions of the thunder beings of the west can act as heyokas. They have sacred power and they share some of this with all the people, but they do it through funny actions."

34 Greenberg, Arthur. *From Alchemy to Chemistry in Picture and Story*. Hoboken, NJ: Wiley-Interscience, 2007. Print.

35 Dry, Sarah. *The Newton Papers: The Strange and True Odyssey of Isaac Newton's Manuscripts*. N.p.: Oxford, 1974. N. pag. Print.

36 Keynes, John Maynard. "Newton, The Man." Ed. Donald Moggridge and Elizabeth Johnson. *Collected Writings of John Maynard Keynes*. Vol. 10. Cambridge, UK: Cambridge UP, 1972. 363–74. Print.

37 Pernety, Antoine-Joseph. "Catalog Record: Dictionnaire Mytho-hermétique, Dans Lequel on Trouve Les Allégories Fabuleuses Des Poètes, Les Métaphores, Les Énigmes Et Les Termes Barbares Des Philosophes Hermétiques Expliqués | Hathi Trust Digital Library." *Catalog Record: Dictionnaire Mytho-hermétique, Dans Lequel...* Public Domain, Google-Digitized, n.d. Web. 21 Nov. 2014. <catalog.hathitrust.org/Record/002888112>.

38 White, Arthur Edward. *Lives of Alchemystical Philosophers: Based on Materials Collected in 1815 and Supplemented by Recent Researches*. London: Redway, 1888. 11–12. Print.

39 Lilly, William. "Book 1." *Christian Astrology Modestly Treated of in Three Books: The First Containing the Use of an Ephemeris, the Erecting of a Scheam of Heaven, Nature of the Twelve Signs of the Zodiack, of the Planets, with a Most Easie Introduction to the Whole Art of Astrology: The Second, by a Most Methodicall Way, Instructeth the Student How to Judge or Resolve All Manner of Questions Contingent Unto Man, Viz., of Health, Sicknesse, Riches, Marriage ...: The Third Containes an Exact Method Whereby to Judge upon Nativities* ... London: Printed by Tho. Brudenell for John Partridge and Humph. Blunden ..., 1647. 48. Print. "The first, tenth, seventh and fourth houses hereof are called Angles, the eleventh, second, eight and fift are called Succedants, the third, twelfth, ninth and sixth are called Cadents: the Angles are most powerful, the Succedants are next in vertue, the Cadents poor and of little efficacy : the Succedants houses follow the angles, Cadents come next the Succedants; in force and vertue they land so in order: 1 10 7 4 11 5 9 3 2 8 6 12."

40 "Trinity." *Trinity*. N.p., n.d. Web. 14 Oct. 2014. <www.nihonbunka.com/shinto/trinity.htm>.

41 Beer, Robert. *The Handbook of Tibetan Buddhist Symbols*. Boston: Shambhala, 2003. 209. Print.

42 Grand unified field: I take the liberty to establish an analogy with this scientific term and take away the capital letters, in hope that some day we can use this wonderful concept as a common reference. In some cases, the act of trivializing can be glorifying.

43 Triality": word composed here on the model of the word "duality", to describe a triangular polarity using a system of three referential points.

44 .Knight, Gareth. "Volume II, Section II, Part I." *A Practical Guide to Qabalistic Symbolism*. Boston: Weiser, 2001. 106. Print. "The Divine seed of Yod recalls to mind the doctrine of the Immaculate Conception."

45 Hamaker-Zondag, Karen. *The Yod Book: Including a Complete Discussion of Unaspected Planets*. York Beach, Me.: Samuel Weiser, 2000. 88. Print.

46 Knight, Gareth. "Volume 1, Part I, Chapter III." *A Practical Guide to Qabalistic Symbolism*. Boston: Weiser, 2001. Fig. 1 (Sephirots) and Fig. 3 (The Pillars). 25 & 27. Print.

47 I use a small capital here to democratize the concept of god, as it might be tired of being capitalized and feared, and the small cap of humility doesn't prevent it from being revered.

48 Iyengar, B. K. S. "The Art of Retention." *Light on Prānāyāma: The Yogic Art of Breathing*. New York: Crossroad, 1981. 106–11. Print.

49 Crone, Hugh D. *Paracelsus: The Man Who Defied Medicine: His Real Contribution to Medicine and Science*. Melbourne: Albarello, 2004. 180. Print.

50 Wang, Robert. *An Introduction to the Golden Dawn Tarot: Including the Original Documents on Tarot from the Order of the Golden Dawn with Explanatory Notes*. York Beach, Me.: S. Weiser, 1978. 34. Print.

51 "GNH INDEX." *Gross National Happiness RSS*. The Centre for Bhutan Studies & GNH Research, n.d. Web. 14 Oct. 2014. <www.grossnationalhappiness.com/articles/>.

52 Attali, Jacques. *A Brief History of the Future: A brave and Controversial Look at the Twenty-first Century*. New York: Arcade Pub., 2009. Print.

53 Laozi, Ong Yi-Ping, and Charles Muller. "Verse 81." *Tao Te Ching*. New York: Barnes & Noble Classics, 2005. 164. Print.

54 Boje, David M. "Theatrics of Leadership?" *Theatrics of Leadership Model*. © David M. Boje, 10 Dec. 2000. Web. 15 Oct. 2014. <business.nmsu.edu/~dboje/teaching/338/leader_model_boje.htm#superman>.

55 I choose to associate the energy of the federative Cancer sign with leadership, which seems to be its higher definition. In some instances,

leading energy is equated to that of the sign of Leo. However Leo's higher purpose is not rulership, which could become self-centered and dictatorial in a low expression, but art and creativity (see Chapter 5).

56 Gandhi, M. K. Trans. Valji Govindji Desai. *Satyagraha in South Africa*. Ahmedabad: Navajivan House, 1928. 109–10. Print.

57 Nelson, Mandela. *Long Walk to Freedom (The Autobiography of Mandela*. N.p.: Little Brown, 1994. 624. Print.

58 Phillips, Donald T. "Speech February 13, 1961." Introduction. *Martin Luther King, Jr., on Leadership: Inspiration & Wisdom for Challenging times*. New York: Warner, 2000. N. pag. Print.

59 Rhea, Ryan. "MLK." *MLK*. N.p., 1999. Web. 14 Oct. 2014. <assemblyseries. wustl.edu/past/MLK.html>.

60 Matofska, Benita. "What Is the Sharing Economy?" *What Is the Sharing Economy?* The People Who Share, n.d. Web. 15 Oct. 2014. <www.thepeoplewhoshare.com/blog/what-is-the-sharing-economy/>.

61 *Towards the Circular Economy*. Isle of Wight: Ellen MacArthur Foundation, 2012. Print.

62 "Cradle to Cradle | The Product-Life Institute." *Cradle to Cradle | The Product-Life Institute*. Product-Life Institute, Geneva, n.d. Web. 15 Oct. 2014. <www.product-life.org/en/cradle-to-cradle>.

63 Pauli, Gunter A. *The Blue Economy 10 Years, 100 Innovations, 100 Million Jobs*. Taos, NM: Paradigm Publications, 2010. Print.

64 Geremek, Bronisław, and Jean Birrell. *The Margins of Society in Late Medieval Paris*. Cambridge: Cambridge UP, 2006. Print. "[...] it was hardly likely that many of these outlaws would be able to establish themselves in a new place, and lead an honest life. Thus, banishment from one town was followed by proscription to another, or from the whole country."

65 "Gurdjieff International Review, Fall 2013, Vol. XII, No. 1." *Gurdjieff International Review*. Gurdjieff Electronic Publishing, n.d. Web. 15 Oct. 2014. <www.gurdjieff.org/>.

66 Keats, John. *ODE TO A GREECIAN URN BY JOHN KEATS*. 54R0613 ed. N.p.: Valenti Angelo, n.d. Print. Hand-press (100 Copies).

67 "J.C Frazer - The Golden Bough." *Anthropology Guide*. N.p., 22 Jan. 2012. Web. 20 Oct. 2014. Frazer, James George. *The Golden Bough: A Study in Magic and Religion*. 3rd ed. London: Macmillan and, Limited, 1912. Print.

68 Campbell, Joseph, Bill D. Moyers, and Betty S. Flowers. *The Power of Myth*. New York: Anchor, 1991. Print. "[...] I came to this idea of bliss because in Sanskrit (the Upanishad) [...] there are three terms that represent the brink, the jumping-off place to the ocean of transcendence:

Sat-Chit-Ananda. The word "Sat" means being. "Chit" means consciousness. "Ananda" means bliss or rapture. I thought, "I don't know whether my consciousness is proper consciousness or not; I don't know whether what I know of my being is my proper being or not; but I do know where my rapture is. So let me hang on to rapture, and that will bring me both my consciousness and my being."

69   The Editors of Encyclopædia Britannica. "Number Theory." *The New Encyclopaedia Brittanica*. 15th ed. Vol. 8. N.p.: n.p., 2003. 827. Print. "Number theory, [...] In ancient times, number theory was associated by numerology, the supposed mystical properties of numbers. This, some writers attached great significance in the coincidence that the biblical Creation took 6 days and that 6 is the smallest "perfect" number – that is, one equal to the sum of its integral factors. Just as during Renaissance astronomy gradually parted company with astrology and chemistry parted from alchemy, so did number theory throw off its association with numerology [...]."

70   Campion, Nicholas. "Classical Greece." *Astrology and Cosmology in the World's Religions*. New York: New York UP, 2012. 125.153. Print.

71   Bell, G., trans. " Book 1, On The Commonwealth." *The Treatises of M. T. Cicero, On the Nature of the Gods; on Divination; On Fate; On The Republic; On The Laws; and On Standing for the Consulship*. N.p.: Google EBook, 1878. 299. Print.

72   Lindsay, Jack. *Origins of Astrology*. New York: Barnes & Noble, 1971. 245. Print.

73   Becker, Robert O., and Gary Selden. *The Body Electric: Electromagnetism and the Foundation of Life*. New York: Morrow, 1985. 247. Print.

74   Paull, John. "Organics Olympiad 2011: Global Indices of Leadership in Organic Agriculture." *Journal of Social and Development Sciences* 1.No. 4 (May 2011): 144–50. orgprints.org/. Institute of Social and Cultural Anthropology, University of Oxford, May 2011. Web. 15 Oct. 2014. <orgprints.org/18860/1/Paull2011OlympiadJSDS.pdf>.

75   Linsay, Jack. "Conclusion." *Origins of Astrology*. New York: Barnes & Noble, 1971. N. pag. Print.

76   Aquinas, Thomas, Saint. "Whether Divination by the Stars Is Unlawful, Part II." *The Summa Theologica of St. Thomas Aquinas, Reginaldeus De Piperno*. Vol. QQ. LXXX -C. Londini: Leland Stanford Junior U, 1922. 200–203. Print.

77   Jung, C. G. "§82." *The Spirit in Man, Art, and Literature*. Vol. 15. Princeton, NJ: Princeton UP, 1971. 56. Print. Bollingen Ser. XX.

78   Barthes, Roland. *Mythologies*. New York: Hill and Wang, 2012. 217. Print.

79 Knight, Gareth. "Volume 1I, Section II, Part I." *A Practical Guide to Qaba-listic Symbolism*. Boston: Weiser, 2001. 104. Print.

80 Echols, Signe E., Robert E. Mueller, and Sandra A. Thomson. *Spiritual Tarot: Seventy-eight Paths to Personal Development*. New York: Avon, 1996. 61–62. Print.

81 Jung, C. G., and R. F. C. Hull. *The Archetypes and the Collective Uncon-scious*. Vol. § 88. Princeton, NJ: Princeton UP, 1980. 42. Print.

82 Ward, Geoff. *Spirals: The Pattern of Existence*. Sutton, Mallet, England: Green Magic, 2006. Print.

83 Iyengar, B. K. S. *Light on Prāṇāyāma: The Yogic Art of Breathing*. New York: Crossroad, 1981. 36. Print. "The word is derived from "kundala", meaning a ring or a coil."

84 "Chief Oren Lyons Opening Statement, "The Year of the Indigenous Peoples" (1993), in the UN General Assembly Auditorium." *Chief Oren Lyons Opening Statement, "The Year of the Indigenous Peoples" (1993), in the UN General Assembly Auditorium*. Trans. Craig Carpenter. N.p., Dec. 2012. Web. 15 Oct. 2014. <www.ratical.org/many_worlds/6Nations/OLa-tUNin92.html>.

85 *The Village*. Dir. M. Knight Shyamalan. Prod. Touchstone Pictures and Blinding Edge Pictures. Buena Vista Pictures, 2004. Film.

86 Russell, Bertrand. "Chapter 6." *The Conquest of Happiness*. N.p.: n.p., n.d. 79–80. Print.

87 Aiyer, Velandai Gopala. *The Chronology of Ancient India: Beginning of the Sat Yuga, Dwaper, Treta, and Kali Yuga with Date of Mahabharata*. Delhi: Sanjay Prakashan, 1987. 127–28. Print.

88 Aquinas, Thomas, St. "Summa Theologica, Volume 1, Part 1, Ques-tion 63, Art. 3. Page 313." *Google Books*. N.p., n.d. Web. 15 Oct. 2014. <books.google.com/books?id=8NV0pNnQrSoC&printsec=frontcover&dq=Summa+Theologica,+Volume+1&hl=en&sa=X&ei=-ro-VMHSEtOgyAT3s4HgDg&ved=0CCYQ6AEwAA#v=onepage&q=Summa%20Theologica%2C%20Volume%201&f=false>.

89 Echols, Signe E., Robert E. Mueller, and Sandra A. Thomson. *Spiritual Tarot: Seventy-eight Paths to Personal Development*. New York: Avon, 1996. 76–77. Print.

90 Echols, Signe E., Robert E. Mueller, and Sandra A. Thomson. *Spiritual Tarot: Seventy-eight Paths to Personal Development*. New York: Avon, 1996. 81–83. Print.

91 Echols, Signe E., Robert E. Mueller, and Sandra A. Thomson. *Spiritual Tarot: Seventy-eight Paths to Personal Development*. New York: Avon, 1996. 78–80. Print.

92 Pound, Ezra, trans. *Confucius, The Unwobbling Pivot & The Great Digest, With Notes and Commentary on the Text and the Ideograms, Together with Ciu His's "Preface" to the Chung Yung and Tseng's Commentary on the Testament.* New York: Pharos, Winter 1947. Print. Number Four.

93 Pound, Ezra, trans. "Part One Tsze Sze's First Thesis, Chapter X Tsze-Lu's Question, Art. 5." *Confucius, The Unwobbling Pivot & The Great Digest, With Notes and Commentary on the Text and the Ideograms, Together with Ciu His's "Preface" to the Chung Yung and Tseng's Commentary on the Testament.* New York: Pharos, Winter 1947. 14. Print. Number Four.

94 Buyya, Rajkumar, James Broberg, and Andrzej Gościński. *Cloud Computing: Principles and Paradigms.* Hoboken, NJ: Wiley, 2011. 16. Print.

95 Vilayat, Inayat Khan Pir, and Pythia Peay. *Thinking like the Universe: The Sufi Path of Awakening.* London: Thorsons, 2000. Print.

96 Vitale, Joe, and Haleakalā Hew Len. *Zero Limits: The Secret Hawaiian System for Wealth, Health, Peace, and More.* Hoboken, NJ: Wiley, 2007. Print.

97 "Online Etymology Dictionary." *Online Etymology Dictionary.* N.p., n.d. Web. 15 Oct. 2014. "Alchemy (n.) mid-14c., from Old French alchimie (14c.), alquemie (13c.), from Medieval Latin alkimia, from Arabic al-kimiya, from Greek khemeioa (found c.300 C.E. in a decree of Diocletian against "the old writings of the Egyptians"), all meaning "alchemy."

98 Steele, Valerie. *Paris Fashion: A Cultural History.* New York: Oxford UP, 1988. 246–48. Print.

99 "Resources for Speakers, Global Issues, Africa, Ageing, Agriculture, Aids, Atomic Energy, Children, Climate Change, Culture, Decolonization, Demining, Development, Disabilities, Disarmament, Environment, Food, Governance, Humanitarian, Refugees, Women." *UN News Center.* UN, n.d. Web. 24 Nov. 2014. <www.un.org/en/globalissues/briefingpapers/endviol/>.

100 Butler, Judith. *Gender Trouble: Feminism and the Subversion of Identity.* New York: Routledge, 1990. Print.

101 "Judith Butler: Your Behavior Creates Your Gender." *YouTube.* YouTube, 13 Jan. 2011. Web. 26 Dec. 2014. <https://www.youtube.com/watch?v=Bo7o2LYATDc>.

102 Gilligan, Carol. *In a Different Voice: Psychological Theory and Women's Development.* Cambridge, MA: Harvard UP, 1982. 8. Print.

103 Noddings, Nel. *Caring, a Feminine Approach to Ethics & Moral Education.* Berkeley: U of California, 1984. Print.

104 Estés, Clarissa Pinkola. *Women Who Run with the Wolves: Myths and Stories of the Wild Woman Archetype.* New York: Ballantine, 1997. 200–01. Print.

105 Woodman, Marion. *The Pregnant Virgin: A Process of Psychological Trans-formation*. Toronto, Canada: Inner City, 1985. 10. Print.

106 Vilayat, Inayat Khan Pir, and Pythia Peay. *Thinking like the Universe: The Sufi Path of Awakening*. London: Thorsons, 2000. 114. Print.

107 Henderson, Joseph L., and Maud Oakes. *The Wisdom of the Serpent: The Myths of Death, Rebirth, and Resurrection*. Princeton, NJ: Princeton UP, 1990. Print.

108 Knight, Gareth. "Volume 1, Part II, Chapter IX." *A Practical Guide to Qabalistic Symbolism*. Boston: Weiser, 2001. 107. Print.

109 Watkins, Thayer H. "Digit Sum Arithmetic." *Digit Sum Arithmetic*. Silicon Valley & Tornado Alley USA, n.d. Web. 15 Oct. 2014.

110 "Genesis Chapter 11 בְּרֵאשִׁית" *Genesis 11 / Hebrew*. Mechon Mamre, n.d. Web. 15 Oct. 2014.

111 Aurelius, Marcus, and George Long. *Meditations*. New York: Barnes & Noble, 2003. 17. Print.

112 "Ecclesiastes Chapter 12 קֹהֶלֶת" *Ecclesiastes 12 / Hebrew*. Mechon Mamre, 2 Feb. 2014. Web. 22 Nov. 2014. <www.mechon-mamre.org/p/pt/pt3112.htm>. 12:6 "Before the silver cord is snapped asunder, and the golden bowl is shattered, and the pitcher is broken at the fountain, and the wheel falleth shattered, into the pit;" 12:7 "And the dust returneth to the earth as it was, and the spirit returneth unto God who gave it."; Smed, Jouni A. "Out-of-Body Experience Studies." *The Monroe Institute*. N.p., n.d. Web. 15 Oct. 2014. <www.monroeinstitute.org/resources/out-of-body-experience-studies>. Silver cord: life thread from the physical to the etheric body felt during out-of-body experiences.

113 "The Revelation of St. John The Divine, 21:12–21:17." *Holy Bible: Authorized King James Version*. Grand Rapids, MI: Zondervan, 2009. 1747–1748. Print.

114 "The Revelation of St. John The Divine, 22:2." *Holy Bible: Authorized King James Version*. Grand Rapids, MI: Zondervan, 2009. 1748. Print.

115 Foucault, Michel. *The Archaelogy of Knowledge And The Discourse on Language*. N.p.: Vintage Books Edition, 2010. 136–37. Print.

116 Fenn, Celia. "Time Travel 101 - Understanding the Radical Shifts of the Last Three Months!" *Starchild Global*. Spirit Library, 7 May 2014. Web. 15 Oct. 2014. <spiritlibrary.com/starchild-global/time-travel-101-understanding-the-radical-shifts-of-the-last-three-months>.

117 Redondo, Roger L., Joshua Kim, Autumn L. Arons, Steve Ramirez, Xu Liu, and Susumu Tonegawa. "Bidirectional Switch of the Valence Associated with a Hippocampal Contextual Memory Engram." *Nature International*

Journal of Science. Nature Publishing Group, 27 Aug. 2014. Web. 2 Feb. 2015. <http%3A%2F%2Fwww.nature.com%2Fnature%2Fjournal%2Fv513%2Fn7518%2Ffull%2Fnature13725.html>.

118 Grinde, Donald A. *The Iroquois and the Founding of the American Nation*. San Francisco: Indian Historian, 1977. 148 & 169. Print.

119 "Health-minded Global Consumers Put Their Money Where Their Mouths Are." *Www.nielsen.com*. The Nielsen Company, 27 Jan. 2015. Web. 3 Feb. 2015. <http%3A%2F%2Fwww.nielsen.com%2Fus%2Fen%2Finsights%2Fnews%2F2015%2Fhealth-minded-global-consumers-put-their-money-where-their-mouths-are.html>.

120 Clark, Patrick. "Counting America's Freelance, Ahem, 'Self-Employed' Workers." *Bloomberg Business Week*. Bloomberg, 10 Sept. 2013. Web. 15 Oct. 2014. <www.businessweek.com/articles/2013–09–10/counting-america-s-freelance-ahem-self-employed-workers>.

121 Rohmann, Chris. "Wave-particle Duality." *A World of Ideas: A Dictionary of Important Theories, Concepts, Beliefs, and Thinkers*. New York: Ballantine, 2000. 425. Print.

122 Einstein, Albert, and Leopold Infeld. *The Evolution of Physics: From Early Concepts to Relativity and Quanta*. New York: Simon and Schuster, 1966. 262–63. Print.

123 Freud, Sigmund, Professor Dr. *Totem and Taboo, Resemblances between the Psychic Lives of Savages and Neurotics*. New York: Moffat Yard, June 1919. Print.

124 Vilayat, Inayat Khan Pir, and Pythia Peay. *Thinking like the Universe: The Sufi Path of Awakening*. London: Thorsons, 2000. 94. Print.

125 Castaneda, Carlos. *The Power of Silence: Further Lessons of Don Juan*. New York: Washington Square, 1991. 3. Print.

126 *Jean-Michel Basquiat: The Radiant Child*. Dir. Tamra Davis, David Koh, Lilly Bright, Stanley Buchthal, and Alexis Manya Spraic. Perf. Jean-Michel Basquiat. Arthouse Films, 2010 (Sundance). Film.

127 Basquiat, Jean Michel. "Basquiat Interviewed by Glenn O'Brien on TV Party."*YouTube*. YouTube, 21 Mar. 2013. Web. 27 Dec. 2014. <https://www.youtube.com/watch?v=EHrZbS1yjmc>.

128 Descartes, René, and Stephen Voss. "First Part, Article 31." *The Passions of the Soul*. Indianapolis: Hackett Pub., 1989. 36–37. Print.

129 Strassman, Rick. *DMT: The Spirit Molecule: A Doctor's Revolutionary Research into the Biology of Near-death and Mystical Experiences*. Rochester, VT: Park Street, 2001. 58–59. Print.

130 Plato, Edith Hamilton, and Huntington Cairns. "Phaedo 79d." Trans.

Hugh Tredennick. *The Collected Dialogues of Plato, including the Letters.* Princeton, NJ: Princeton UP, 1961. 62–63. Print. Bollingen Ser. LXXI.

131 Kryon. "KRYON - United Nations 2009." *KRYON - United Nations 2009.* N.p., n.d. Web. 15 Oct. 2014. <kryon.com/k_65.html>.

132 Kryon. "San Antonio, Texas - February 22, 2014." *San Antonio, Texas - February 22, 2014.* N.p., 22 Feb. 2014. Web. 15 Oct. 2014. <www.kryon.com/CHAN2014/k_channel14_SANANTONIO-14.html>.

133 "How Much Water Is There On, In, and above the Earth?" *How Much Water Is There on Earth, from the USGS Water Science School.* U.S. Department of the Interior, n.d. Web. 12 Oct. 2014.

134 Emoto, Masaru. *The Hidden Messages in Water.* Hillsboro, Or.: Beyond Words Pub., 2004. Print.

135 DeWoody, Jennifer, Carol A. Rowe, Valerie D. Hipkins, and Karen E. Mock. ""Pando" Lives: Molecular Genetic Evidence of a Giant Aspen Clone in Central Utah." *BioOne.* Western North American Naturalist, n.d. Web. 15 Oct. 2014. <www.bioone.org/doi/abs/10.3398/1527-0904-68.4.493>.

136 "Abundant Number | Planetmath.org." *Abundant Number | Planetmath.org.* Planetmath.org, n.d. Web. 15 Oct. 2014. <planetmath.org/AbundantNumber>.

137 Koestler, Arthur. *The Ghost in the Machine.* London: Arkana, 1989. 58. Print.

138 Laureyssens, Dirk. "Holism and the Creation of Holons." *Holism and the Creation of Holons.* Big Tube Theory, n.d. Web. 15 Oct. 2014. <www.mu6.com/holon_causality.html>.

139 Saint-Exupéry, Antoine De, and Richard Howard. *The Little Prince.* San Diego: Harcourt, 2000. 63. Print.

140 Augustine, and Roland J. Teske. "§ 7." *Saint Augustine on Genesis: Two Books on Genesis against the Manichees ; And, On the Literal Interpretation of Genesis, an Unfinished Book.* Washington: Catholic U of America, 1991. 54. Print.

141 Finnis, John. "Aquinas' Moral, Political, and Legal Philosophy." *Stanford University.* Stanford University, 02 Dec. 2005. Web. 15 Oct. 2014.

142 Small, Jacquelyn. *Psyche's Seeds: The Twelve Sacred Principles of Soul-based Psychology.* New York: J.P. Tarcher/Putnam, 2001. Print.

143 Jung, C. G., and R. F. C. Hull. *The Archetypes and the Collective Unconscious.* Princeton, NJ: Princeton UP, 1980. 357. Print.

144 Look, Brandon C. "Gottfried Wilhelm Leibniz." *Stanford University.* Stanford University, 22 Dec. 2007. Web. 15 Oct. 2014.

SOURCES

BIBLIOGRAPHY

Aiyer, Velandai Gopala. *The Chronology of Ancient India: Beginning of the Sat Yuga, Dwaper, Treta, and Kali Yuga with Date of Mahabharata*. Delhi: Sanjay Prakashan, 1987.

Aquinas, Thomas, Saint. "Whether Divination by the Stars Is Unlawful, Part II." *The Summa Theologica of St. Thomas Aquinas, Reginaldeus De Piperno*. Vol. QQ. LXXX -C. Londini: Leland Stanford Junior U, 1922. Print.

Aristotle. *"XVII METAPHYSICS I-IXNYPL"*. N.p.: Research Libraries 3 3433 07673217 5, n.d. 2+.

Attali, Jacques. *A Brief History of the Future: A brave and Controversial Look at the Twenty-first Century*. New York: Arcade Pub, 2009.

Augustine, and Roland J. Teske. "§ 7." *Saint Augustine on Genesis: Two Books on Genesis against the Manichees ; And, On the Literal Interpretation of Genesis, an Unfinished Book*. Washington: Catholic U of America, 1991.

Aurelius, Marcus, and George Long. *Meditations*. New York: Barnes & Noble, 2003. 17.

Barthes, Roland. *Mythologies*. New York: Hill and Wang, 2012.

Becker, Robert O., and Gary Selden. *The Body Electric: Electromagnetism and the Foundation of Life*. New York: Morrow, 1985.

Beer, Robert. *The Handbook of Tibetan Buddhist Symbols*. Boston: Shambhala, 2003.

Bell, G., trans. " Book 1, On The Commonwealth." *The Treatises of M. T. Cicero, On the Nature of the Gods; on Divination; On Fate; On The Republic; On The Laws; and On Standing for the Consulship*. N.p.: Google EBook, 1878.

Butler, Judith. *Gender Trouble: Feminism and the Subversion of Identity*. New York: Routledge, 1990.

Buyya, Rajkumar, James Broberg, and Andrzej Gościński. *Cloud Computing: Principles and Paradigms*. Hoboken, NJ: Wiley, 2011.

Campbell, Joseph, Bill D. Moyers, and Betty S. Flowers. *The Power of Myth*. New York: Anchor, 1991.

Campion, Nicholas. "Classical Greece." *Astrology and Cosmology in the World's Religions*. New York: New York UP, 2012. Print.

Castaneda, Carlos. *The Power of Silence: Further Lessons of Don Juan*. New York: Washington Square, 1991.

Crone, Hugh D. *Paracelcus: The Man Who Defied Medicine: His Real Contribution to Medicine and Science*. Melbourne: Albarello, 2004.

Dean, Bartholomew. *Urarina Society, Cosmology, and History in Peruvian Amazonia*. Gainesville: U of Florida, 2009.

Descartes, René, and Stephen Voss. "First Part, Article 31." *The Passions of the Soul*. Indianapolis: Hackett Pub, 1989.

Dry, Sarah. *The Newton Papers: The Strange and True Odyssey of Isaac Newton's Manuscripts*. N.p.: Oxford, 1974.

Echols, Signe E., Robert E. Mueller, and Sandra A. Thomson. *Spiritual Tarot: Seventy-eight Paths to Personal Development*. New York: Avon, 1996.

Einstein, Albert, and Leopold Infeld. *The Evolution of Physics: From Early Concepts to Relativity and Quanta*. New York: Simon and Schuster, 1966.

Elk, Black, and John Gneisenau Neihardt. *Black Elk Speaks: Being the Life Story of a Holy Man of the Oglala Sioux*. Lincoln: U of Nebraska, 1988.

Emoto, Masaru. *The Hidden Messages in Water*. Hillsboro, Or.: Beyond Words Pub., 2004.

Epictetus, and Robert F. Dobbin. "Book 1, Chapter 15, What Philosophy Professes." *Discourses and Selected Writings*. London: Penguin, 2008.

Escher, M. C. *The Magic of M. C. Escher*. N.p.: Thames & Hudson, 2000. Print. Reprinted 2006.

Estés, Clarissa Pinkola. *Women Who Run with the Wolves: Myths and Stories of the Wild Woman Archetype*. New York: Ballantine, 1997.

Foucault, Michel. *The Archaelogy of Knowledge And The Discourse on Language*. N.p.: Vintage Books Edition, 2010.

Freud, Sigmund, Professor Dr. *Totem and Taboo, Resemblances between the Psychic Lives of Savages and Neurotics*. New York: Moffat Yard, June 1919.

Gandhi, M. K. Trans. Valji Govindji Desai. *Satyagraha in South Africa*. Ahmedabad: Navajivan House, 1928.

Geremek, Bronisław, and Jean Birrell. *The Margins of Society in Late Medieval Paris*. Cambridge: Cambridge UP, 2006.

Gilligan, Carol. *In a Different Voice: Psychological Theory and Women's Development*. Cambridge, MA: Harvard UP, 1982.

Greenberg, Arthur. *From Alchemy to Chemistry in Picture and Story*. Hoboken, NJ: Wiley-Interscience, 2007.

Grinde, Donald A. *The Iroquois and the Founding of the American Nation*. San Francisco: Indian Historian, 1977.

Hamaker-Zondag, Karen. *The Yod Book: Including a Complete Discussion of Unaspected Planets*. York Beach, Me.: Samuel Weiser, 2000.

Henderson, Joseph L., and Maud Oakes. *The Wisdom of the Serpent: The Myths of Death, Rebirth, and Resurrection*. Princeton, NJ: Princeton UP, 1990.

Iyengar, B. K. S. *Light on Prāṇāyāma: The Yogic Art of Breathing*. New York: Crossroad, 1981.

"J.C Frazer - The Golden Bough." *Anthropology Guide*. N.p., 22 Jan. 2012. Web. 20 Oct. 2014. Frazer, James George. *The Golden Bough: A Study in Magic and Religion*. 3rd ed. London: Macmillan and, Limited, 1912.

Jung, C. G., and R. F. C. Hull. *The Archetypes and the Collective Unconscious*. Princeton, NJ: Princeton UP, 1980.

Jung, C. G. "§82." *The Spirit in Man, Art, and Literature*. Vol. 15. Princeton, NJ: Princeton UP, 1971. 56. Print. Bollingen Ser. XX.

Keats, John. *ODE TO A GREECIAN URN BY JOHN KEATS*. 54R0613 ed. N.p.: Valenti Angelo, n.d. Print. Hand-press (100 Copies).

Keynes, John Maynard. "Newton, The Man." Ed. Donald Moggridge and Elizabeth Johnson. *Collected Writings of John Maynard Keynes*. Vol. 10. Cambridge, UK: Cambridge UP, 1972.

King, Leonard William. *The Seven Tablets of Creation, or the Babylonian and Assyrian Legends concerning the Creation of the World and of Mankind, Edited by L. W. King,..* London: Luzac, 1902. Print; Reiner, Erica. "Part 2: Enuma Any Enlil." *Babylonian Planetary Omens*. Malibu: Undena Publ., 1981. Tablets 50–51.

Knight, Gareth. "Volume 1, Part I, Chapter III." *A Practical Guide to Qabalistic Symbolism*. Boston: Weiser, 2001.

Koestler, Arthur. *The Ghost in the Machine*. London: Arkana, 1989.

Laozi, Ong Yi-Ping, and Charles Muller. "Verse 81." *Tao Te Ching*. New York: Barnes & Noble Classics, 2005.

Lilly, William. "Book 1." *Christian Astrology Modestly Treated of in Three Books: The First Containing the Use of an Ephemeris, the Erecting of a Scheam of Heaven, Nature of the Twelve Signs of the Zodiack, of the Planets, with a Most Easie Introduction to the Whole Art of Astrology: The Second, by a Most Methodicall Way, Instructeth the Student How to Judge or Resolve All Manner of Questions Contingent Unto Man, Viz., of Health, Sicknesse, Riches, Marriage ...: The Third Containes an Exact Method Whereby to Judge upon Nativities ...* London: Printed by Tho. Brudenell for John Partridge and Humph. Blunden ..., 1647.

Lindsay, Jack. *Origins of Astrology*. New York: Barnes & Noble, 1971.

Monroe, Robert A. *Far Journeys*. Garden City, NY: Doubleday, 1985.

Nelson, Mandela. *Long Walk to Freedom (The Autobiography of Mandela*. N.p.: Little Brown, 1994.

Noddings, Nel. *Caring, a Feminine Approach to Ethics & Moral Education*. Berkeley: U of California, 1984.

Pauli, Gunter A. *The Blue Economy 10 Years, 100 Innovations, 100 Million Jobs*. Taos, NM: Paradigm Publications, 2010.

Peters, F. E. *Greek Philosophical Terms; a Historical Lexicon*. New York: New York UP, 1967.

Phillips, Donald T. "Speech February 13, 1961." Introduction. *Martin Luther King, Jr., on Leadership: Inspiration & Wisdom for Challenging times*. New York: Warner, 2000.

Pingree, David Edwin, and Reiner, Erica. "Enlil, Enûma Anu." "Part 1: The Venus Tablet of Ammisaduqa, Enuma Anu Enlil." *Babylonian Planetary Omens*. Malibu, Calif: Undena Publ., 1975. Tablet 63.

Platon, and Paul Shorey. *The Republic*. London: William Heinemann, 1963. Print. Aristotle, and David Keyt. *Politics*. Oxford: Clarendon, 1999.

Plato, Edith Hamilton, and Huntington Cairns. "Timaeus Dialogue, 53c3–6, 54cd, 55abc." *The Collected Dialogues of Plato, including the Letters*. Princeton, NJ: Princeton UP, 1961. 1180–181. Print. Bollingen Ser. LXXI.

Pound, Ezra, trans. *Confucius, The Unwobbling Pivot & The Great Digest, With Notes and Commentary on the Text and the Ideograms, Together with Ciu His's "Preface" to the Chung Yung and Tseng's Commentary on the Testament*. New York: Pharos, Winter 1947. Number Four.

Rohmann, Chris. "Wave-particle Duality." *A World of Ideas: A Dictionary of Important Theories, Concepts, Beliefs, and Thinkers*. New York: Ballantine, 2000.

Russell, Bertrand. "Chapter 6." *The Conquest of Happiness*. N.p.: n.p., n.d.

Saint-Exupéry, Antoine De, and Richard Howard. *The Little Prince*. San Diego: Harcourt, 2000.

Schopenhauer, Arthur. *The World as Will and Idea*. London: Everyman, 2004.

Small, Jacquelyn. *Psyche's Seeds: The Twelve Sacred Principles of Soul-based Psychology*. New York: J.P. Tarcher/Putnam, 2001.

Steele, Valerie. *Paris Fashion: A Cultural History*. New York: Oxford UP, 1988.

Strassman, Rick. *DMT: The Spirit Molecule: A Doctor's Revolutionary Research into the Biology of Near-death and Mystical Experiences*. Rochester, VT: Park Street, 2001.

The Editors of Encyclopædia Britannica. "Number Theory." *The New Encyclopaedia Brittanica*. 15th ed. Vol. 8. N.p.: n.p., 2003.

"The Revelation of St. John The Divine" *Holy Bible: Authorized King James Version*. Grand Rapids, MI: Zondervan, 2009.

Towards the Circular Economy. Isle of Wight: Ellen MacArthur Foundation, 2012.

Vilayat, Inayat Khan Pir, and Pythia Peay. *Thinking like the Universe: The Sufi Path of Awakening*. London: Thorsons, 2000.

Vitale, Joe, and Haleakalā Hew Len. *Zero Limits: The Secret Hawaiian System for Wealth, Health, Peace, and More*. Hoboken, NJ: Wiley, 2007.

Wang, Robert. *An Introduction to the Golden Dawn Tarot: Including the Original Documents on Tarot from the Order of the Golden Dawn with Explanatory Notes*. York Beach, Me.: S. Weiser, 1978.

Ward, Geoff. *Spirals: The Pattern of Existence*. Sutton, Mallet, England: Green Magic, 2006.

White, Arthur Edward. *Lives of Alchemystical Philosophers: Based on Materials Collected in 1815 and Supplemented by Recent Researches*. London: Redway, 1888.

Woodman, Marion. *The Pregnant Virgin: A Process of Psychological Transformation*. Toronto, Canada: Inner City, 1985.

ONLINE RESOURCES
WEB ARTICLES

"Abraham Lincoln's Crucial Formative Years." *History Press Blog*. N.p., 12 Nov. 2012. Web. 14 Oct. 2014. <www.historypressblog.net/2012/11/27/abraham-lincolns-formative-years/>.

"Abundant Number | Planetmath.org." *Abundant Number | Planetmath. org*. Planetmath.org, n.d. Web. 15 Oct. 2014. <planetmath.org/AbundantNumber>.

Aquinas, Thomas, St. "Summa Theologica, Volume 1, Part 1, Question 63, Art. 3. Page 313." *Google Books*. N.p., n.d. Web. 15 Oct. 2014. <books.google.com/books?id=8NVOpNnQrSoC&printsec=frontcover&dq=Summa+Theologica,+Volume+1&hl=en&sa=X&ei=-ro-VMHSEtOgyAT3s4HgDg&ved=0CCYQ6AEwAA#v=onepage&q=Summa%20Theologica%2C%20Volume%201&f=false>.

Bamon, Leopoldo Garcia. "Correspondance; Le Noel En Espagne." *Le Monde Illustre* 12.15 (1871): 402. *Google Books*. Web. 14 Oct. 2014.

Boje, David M. "Theatrics of Leadership?" *Theatrics of Leadership Model*. © David M. Boje, 10 Dec. 2000. Web. 15 Oct. 2014. <business.nmsu.edu/~dboje/teaching/338/leader_model_boje.htm#superman>.

"Chief Oren Lyons Opening Statement, "The Year of the Indigenous Peoples" (1993), in the UN General Assembly Auditorium." *Chief Oren Lyons Opening Statement, "The Year of the Indigenous Peoples" (1993), in the UN General Assembly Auditorium*. Trans. Craig Carpenter. N.p., Dec. 2012. Web. 15 Oct. 2014. <www.ratical.org/many_worlds/6Nations/OLatUNin92.html>.

Clark, Patrick. "Counting America's Freelance, Ahem, 'Self-Employed' Workers." *Bloomberg Business Week*. Bloomberg, 10 Sept. 2013. Web. 15 Oct. 2014. <www.businessweek.com/articles/2013-09-10/counting-america-s-freelance-ahem-self-employed-workers>.

Covert, Bryce. "CEOs Earn Nearly 300 Times What Their Workers Make." *Think Progress RSS*. N.p., 12 June 2014. Web. 18 Nov. 2014.

"Cradle to Cradle | The Product-Life Institute." *Cradle to Cradle | The Product-Life Institute*. Product-Life Institute, Geneva, n.d. Web. 15 Oct. 2014. <www.product-life.org/en/cradle-to-cradle>.

"Definition of Space-time in English:." *Space-time: Definition of Space-time in Oxford Dictionary (American English) (US)*. N.p., n.d. Web. 14 Oct. 2014. <www.oxforddictionaries.com/us/definition/american_english/space-time>.

"Definition of Singularity in English:." *Singularity: Definition of Singularity in Oxford Dictionary (British & World English)*. N.p., n.d. Web. 14 Oct. 2014. <www.oxforddictionaries.com/definition/english/singularity>.

DeWoody, Jennifer, Carol A. Rowe, Valerie D. Hipkins, and Karen E. Mock. ""Pando" Lives: Molecular Genetic Evidence of a Giant Aspen Clone in Central Utah." *BioOne*. Western North American Naturalist, n.d. Web. 15 Oct. 2014. <www.bioone.org/doi/abs/10.3398/1527–0904–68.4.493>.

Diep, Francie. "An All-Liquid Battery For Storing Solar And Wind Energy."*Popular Science*. N.p., 2 Sept. 2014. Web. 19 Nov. 2014.

"Ecclesiastes Chapter 12 תְּלֶהֹק." *Ecclesiastes 12 / Hebrew*. Mechon Mamre, 2 Feb. 2014. Web. 22 Nov. 2014. <www.mechon-mamre.org/p/pt/pt3112.htm>.

"EMF Pollution from Living Near Power Lines - Solved?" *EMF Pollution from Living Near Power Lines - Solved?* Dimensional Design Products, Inc., 2013. Web. 14 Oct. 2014.

Fenn, Celia. "Time Travel 101 - Understanding the Radical Shifts of the Last Three Months!" *Starchild Global*. Spirit Library, 7 May 2014. Web. 15 Oct. 2014. <spiritlibrary.com/starchild-global/time-travel-101-understanding-the-radical-shifts-of-the-last-three-months>.

"File:Klein Bottle.svg." - *Wikimedia Commons*. Free Software Foundation, n.d. Web. 03 Feb. 2015.

Finnis, John. "Aquinas' Moral, Political, and Legal Philosophy." *Stanford University*. Stanford University, 02 Dec. 2005. Web. 15 Oct. 2014.

"Genesis Chapter 11 תִּישְׁאָרְב." *Genesis 11 / Hebrew*. Mechon Mamre, n.d. Web. 15 Oct. 2014.

"GNH INDEX." *Gross National Happiness RSS*. The Centre for Bhutan Studies & GNH Research, n.d. Web. 14 Oct. 2014. <www.grossnationalhappiness.com/articles/>.

"Gurdjieff International Review, Fall 2013, Vol. XII, No. 1." *Gurdjieff International Review*. Gurdjieff Electronic Publishing, n.d. Web. 15 Oct. 2014. <www.gurdjieff.org/>.

"Health-minded Global Consumers Put Their Money Where Their Mouths Are." *Www.nielsen.com*. The Nielsen Company, 27 Jan. 2015. Web. 3 Feb. 2015. nielsen.com/us/en/insights/news/2015/health-minded-global-consumers-put-their-money-where-their-mouths-are.html.

Inwagen, Peter Van. "Metaphysics." *Stanford University*. Stanford University, 10 Sept. 2007. Web. 14 Oct. 2014.

Jackson, Michael. "Michael Jackson Interview with GetMusic.com - Part 1, 2:12–2:59." *YouTube*. Ed. Anthony DeCurtis. YouTube, 26 Oct. 2001. Web. 15 Oct. 2014.

Keller, Michael. "Key To LED Lighting Revolution Wins Three Physics Nobel." *Txchnologist*. General Electric, 7 Oct. 2014. Web. 19 Nov. 2014.

Knapp, Alex. "A Black Hole Brings New Stars To Life." *Forbes*. Forbes Magazine, n.d. Web. 14 Oct. 2014. <www.forbes.com/sites/alexknapp/2012/02/07/a-black-hole-brings-new-stars-to-life/>.

Kryon. "KRYON - United Nations 2009." *KRYON - United Nations 2009*. N.p., n.d. Web. 15 Oct. 2014. <kryon.com/k_65.html>.

Kryon. "San Antonio, Texas - February 22, 2014." *San Antonio, Texas - February 22, 2014*. N.p., 22 Feb. 2014. Web. 15 Oct. 2014. <www.kryon.com/CHAN2014/k_channel14_SANANTONIO-14.html>.

"How Much Water Is There On, In, and above the Earth?" *How Much Water Is There on Earth, from the USGS Water Science School*. U.S. Department of the Interior, n.d. Web. 12 Oct. 2014.

Laureyssens, Dirk. "Holism and the Creation of Holons." *Holism and the Creation of Holons*. Big Tube Theory, n.d. Web. 15 Oct. 2014. <www.mu6.com/holon_causality.html>.

Look, Brandon C. "Gottfried Wilhelm Leibniz." *Stanford University*. Stanford University, 22 Dec. 2007. Web. 15 Oct. 2014.

Matofska, Benita. "What Is the Sharing Economy?" *What Is the Sharing Economy?* The People Who Share, n.d. Web. 15 Oct. 2014. <www.thepeoplewhoshare.com/blog/what-is-the-sharing-economy/>.

"Online Etymology Dictionary." *Online Etymology Dictionary*. N.p., n.d. Web. 15 Oct. 2014.

Paull, John. "Organics Olympiad 2011: Global Indices of Leadership in Organic Agriculture." *Journal of Social and Development Sciences* 1.No. 4 (May 2011): 144–50. *orgprints.org/*. Institute of Social and Cultural Anthropology, University of Oxford, May 2011. Web. 15 Oct. 2014. <orgprints.org/18860/1/Paull2011OlympiadJSDS.pdf>.

Pernety, Antoine-Joseph. "Catalog Record: Dictionnaire Mytho-hermétique, Dans Lequel on Trouve Les Allégories Fabuleuses Des Poètes, Les Métaphores, Les Énigmes Et Les Termes Barbares Des Philosophes Hermétiques Expliqués | Hathi Trust Digital Library." *Catalog Record: Dictionnaire Mytho-hermétique, Dans Lequel...* Public Domain, Google-Digitized, n.d. Web. 21 Nov. 2014. <catalog.hathitrust.org/Record/002888112>.

Redondo, Roger L., Joshua Kim, Autumn L. Arons, Steve Ramirez, Xu Liu, and Susumu Tonegawa. "Bidirectional Switch of the Valence Associated with a Hippocampal Contextual Memory Engram." *Nature International Journal of Science*. Nature Publishing Group, 27 Aug. 2014. Web. 2 Feb. 2015. <www.nature.com/nature/journal/v513/n7518/full/nature13725.html>.

"Resources for Speakers, Global Issues, Africa, Ageing, Agriculture, Aids, Atomic Energy, Children, Climate Change, Culture, Decolonization, Demining, Development, Disabilities, Disarmament, Environment, Food, Governance, Humanitarian, Refugees, Women." *UN News Center*. UN, n.d. Web. 24 Nov. 2014. <www.un.org/en/globalissues/briefingpapers/endviol/>.

Rhea, Ryan. "MLK." *MLK*. N.p., 1999. Web. 14 Oct. 2014. <assemblyseries. wustl.edu/past/MLK.html>.

Rosaler, Josh. "The Oxonian Review » An Interview with Brian Greene." *The Oxonian Review RSS*. The Oxonian Review, 4 Apr. 2011. Web. 14 Oct. 2014.

Salford, Leif G., Arne E. Brun, Jacob L. Eberhardt, Lars Malmgren, and Bertil R. R. Persson. "Abstract." *National Center for Biotechnology Information*. U.S. National Library of Medicine, 22 Nov. 0005. Web. 14 Oct. 2014.

Smed, Jouni A. "Out-of-Body Experience Studies." *The Monroe Institute*. N.p., n.d. Web. 15 Oct. 2014. <www.monroeinstitute.org/resources/out-of-body-experience-studies>.

The Editors of Encyclopædia Britannica. "Absolute Idealism (philosophy)." *Encyclopedia Britannica Online*. Encyclopedia Britannica, n.d. Web. 14 Oct. 2014.

The Editors of Encyclopædia Britannica. "Tat Tvam Asi (Hinduism)." *Encyclopedia Britannica Online*. Encyclopedia Britannica, n.d. Web. 14 Oct. 2014.

The Editors of Encyclopædia Britannica. "Wujing (Chinese Texts)." *Encyclopedia Britannica Online*. Encyclopedia Britannica, n.d. Web. 14 Oct. 2014.

"Trinity." *Trinity*. N.p., n.d. Web. 14 Oct. 2014. <www.nihonbunka.com/shinto/trinity.htm>.

Wang, Kangli, Kai Jiang, Brice Chung, Takanari Ouchi, Paul J. Burke, Dane A. Boysen, David J. Bradwell, Hojong Kim, Ulrich Muecke, and Donald R. Sadoway. "Lithium–antimony–lead Liquid Metal Battery for Grid-level Energy Storage." *Nature.com*. N.p., 16 Oct. 2014. Web. 19 Nov. 2014.

Watkins, Thayer H. "Digit Sum Arithmetic." *Digit Sum Arithmetic*. Silicon Valley & Tornado Alley USA, n.d. Web. 15 Oct. 2014.

Film/Audio

Basquiat, Jean Michel. "Basquiat Interviewed by Glenn O'Brien on TV Party." *YouTube*. YouTube, 21 Mar. 2013. Web. 27 Dec. 2014. <www.youtube.com/watch?v=EHrZbS1yjmc>.

Jean-Michel Basquiat: The Radiant Child. Dir. Tamra Davis, David Koh, Lilly Bright, Stanley Buchthal, and Alexis Manya Spraic. Perf. Jean-Michel Basquiat. Arthouse Films, 2010 (Sundance). Film.

Jones, Grace. By Bruce Woolley, Simon Darlow, Steven Lipson, and Trevor Horn. *Slaves to the Rhythm*. Grace Jones. Horn, 1985. CD.

"Judith Butler: Your Behavior Creates Your Gender." *YouTube*. YouTube, 13 Jan. 2011. Web. 26 Dec. 2014. <www.youtube.com/watch?v=Bo7o2LYATDc>.

The Village. Dir. M. Knight Shyamalan. Prod. Touchstone Pictures and Blinding Edge Pictures. Buena Vista Pictures, 2004. Film.

ACKNOWLEDGEMENTS

Heartfelt thanks to Jeanne Kessira, Elisabeth et Philippe Linard, Marie Thérèse De Belder, Thomas Jamet, Roland Legiardi-Laura, J.J. Blick-stein, Clothilde Jamet, Laurence Singer, Sheila Buff, Lidewij Edelkoort, and all of you who are supporting this co-creation, in spirit or else. It is only beginning.

CPSIA information can be obtained at www.ICGtesting.com
Printed in the USA
BVOW05s0026100415

395570BV00002BA/2/P